THE CAMBODIAN JOURNAL

THE CAMBODIAN JOURNAL
DRAWINGS 1994-1998

by Valentina DuBasky

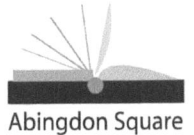

Abingdon Square

The Cambodian Journal Drawings 1994-1998
published by
Abingdon Square Publishing
463 West Street, Suite G122
New York, NY 10014
USA
(212) 691-2543
info@abingdonsquarepublishing.com
www.abingdonsquarepublishing.com

ISBN 978-0-9823480-1-7
Library of Congress Control Number: 2009928118

First Printing: June 2009
Printed in the United States of America

Book design: Abingdon Square Publishing

A Khmer language edition of this publication is available through Abingdon Square Publishing.

cover: *Tragic Harvest: Landmines in his Field,* ink on paper, 8 x 7.25 inches, 1996

This book is dedicated to the people of Cambodia,
with gratitude and respect.

TABLE OF CONTENTS

INTRODUCTION

THE CAMBODIAN JOURNAL is a book of drawings that traces my journey in Cambodia between 1994, after the cease fire ended the long civil war and established a fragile democracy, and the first Cambodian National Elections in 1998. It was a journey taken among survivors of the Khmer Rouge genocide that claimed over a million and a half lives. Through the artwork, I have tried to bear witness to both the trauma of war and the journey of recovery; to the complexity of Cambodia's recent history and the simplicity of being present. The events depicted in the drawings have been inspired by Cambodian friends, colleagues and companions who shared their stories and by encounters with remarkable people whose efforts make a difference. In some of the drawings I respond to briefings and fact-finding trips to the field, record observations of daily life and reflect on personal experiences in Phnom Penh and the countryside. Two of the drawings describe travels farther afield in Laos and Vietnam. As the Cambodian people rebuilt their shattered communities, I discovered the resiliency of the human spirit under extraordinary circumstances and the capacity of art to offer new ways of seeing and understanding.

—Valentina DuBasky
New York, 2009

IMAGINE

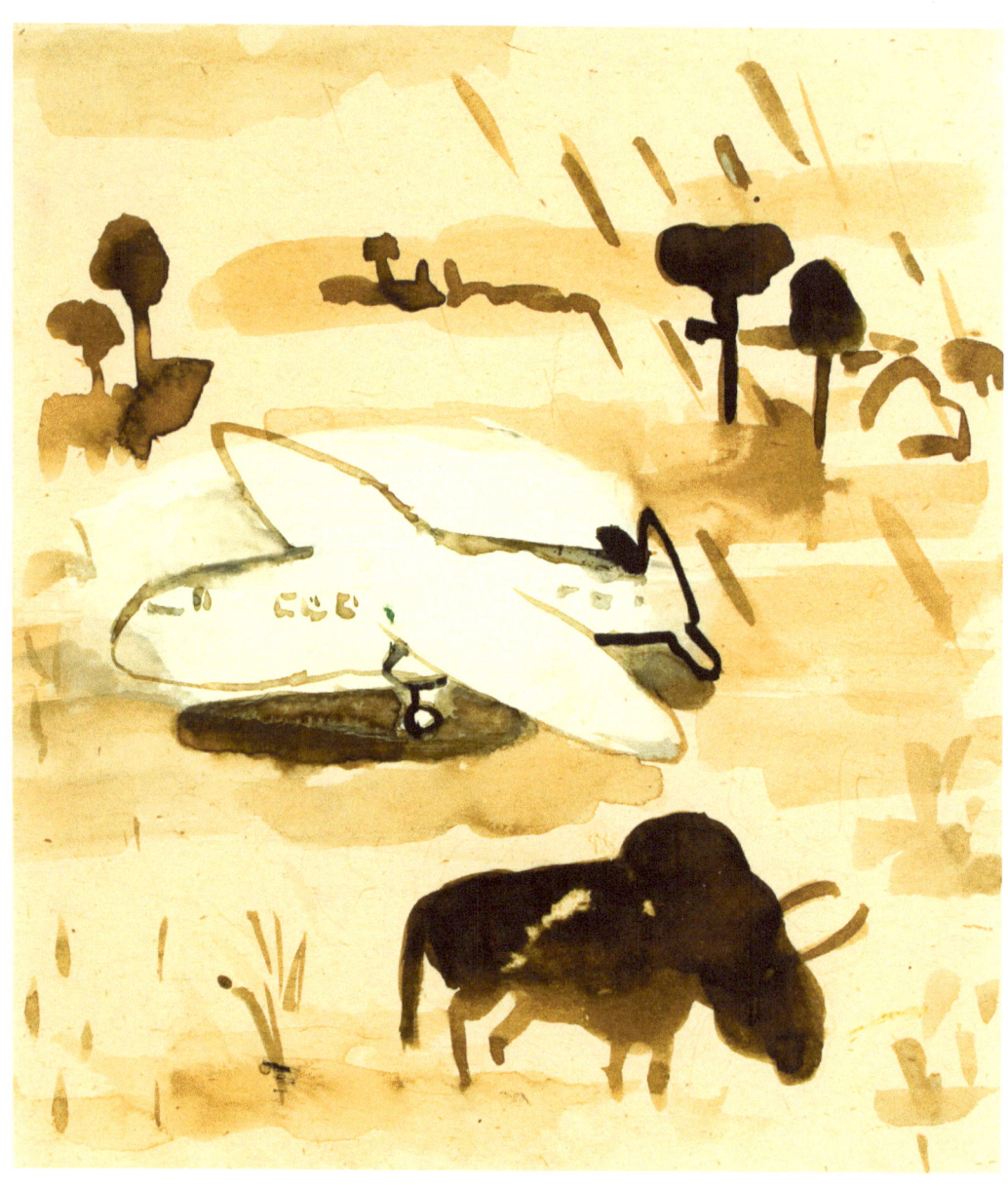

Flying into Battambang

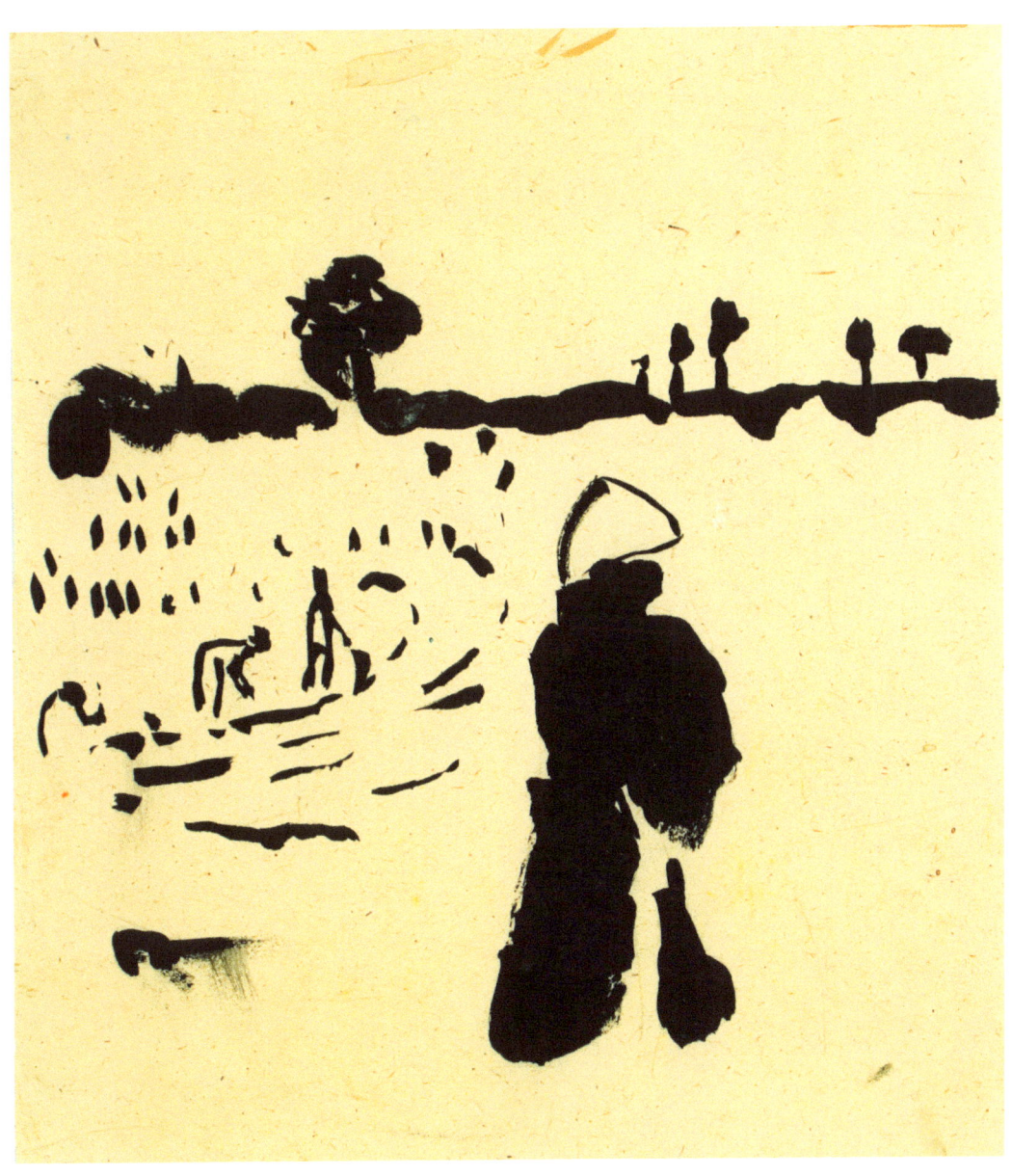

Rice Fields

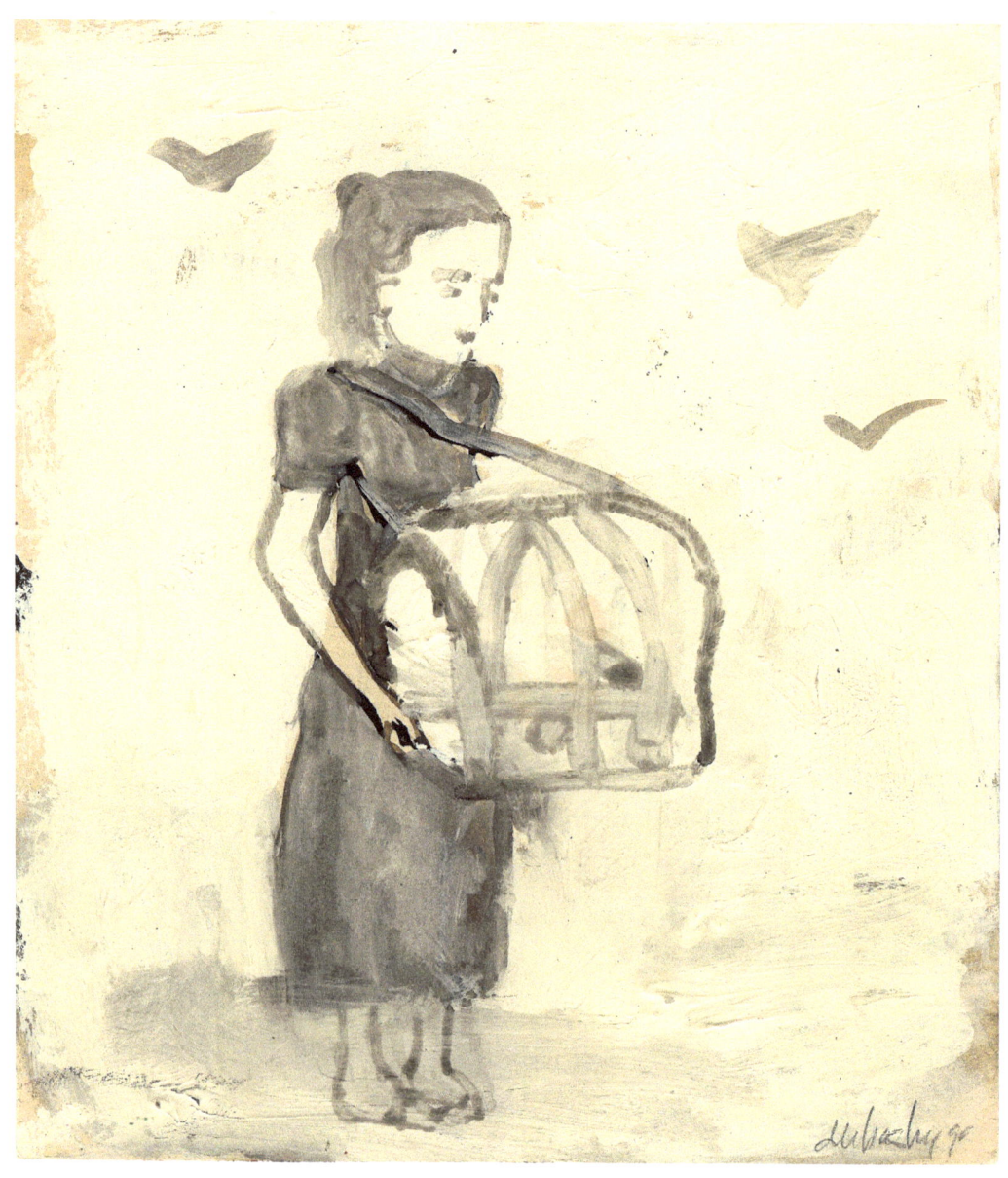

The Little Bird Seller
The little bird seller walks on the banks of the Mekong River. You can buy a small bird
from her so that you can release it to gain merit for a better rebirth.

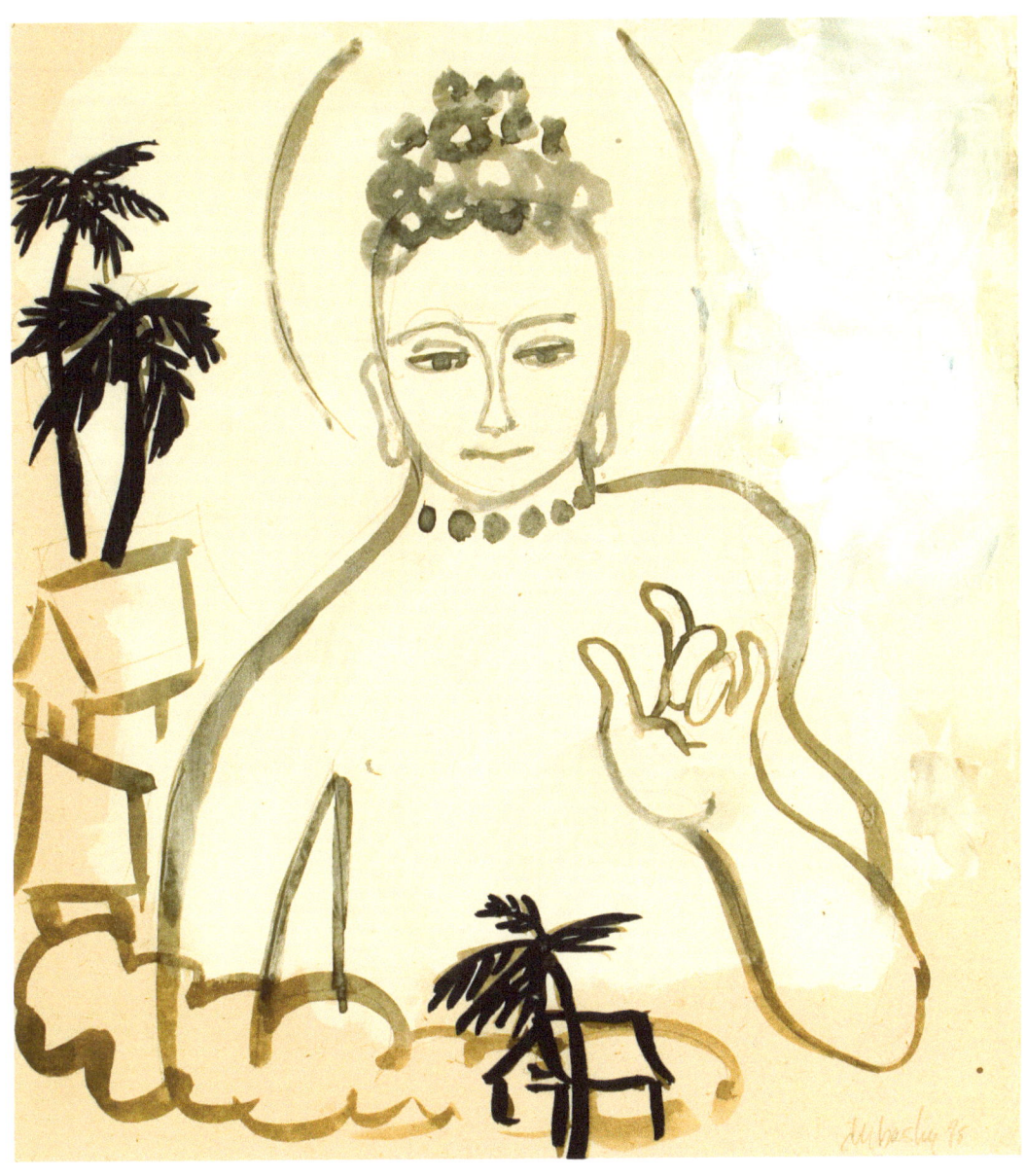

The Thieves Pagoda
The Khmer Rouge torched this once-elegant Buddhist temple. Today a community
of squatters live in the ruins and it is now called the Thieves Pagoda.

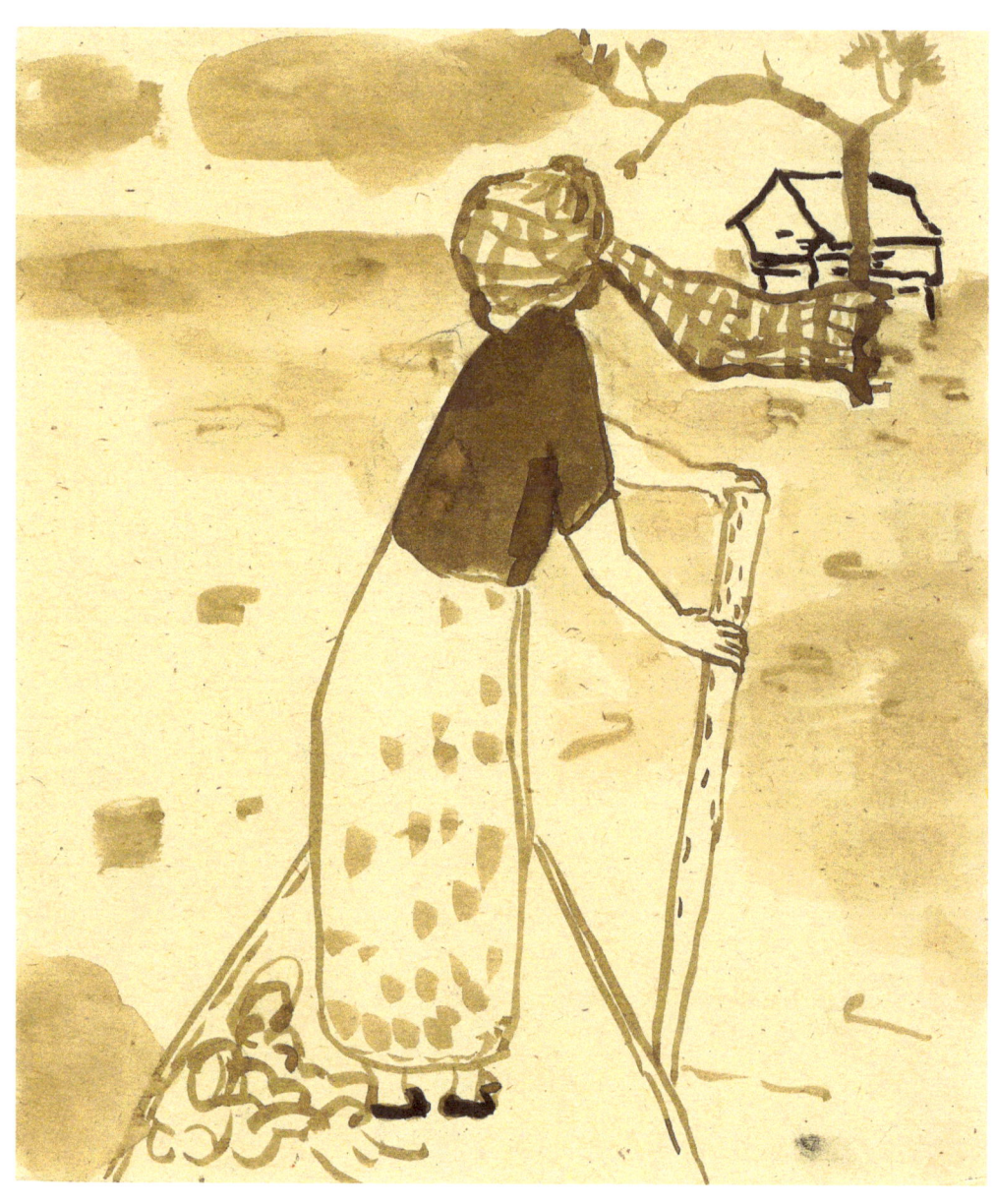

"I think we knew each other in a past life."
— *Halimas, a Cham fisherwoman*

SORROW

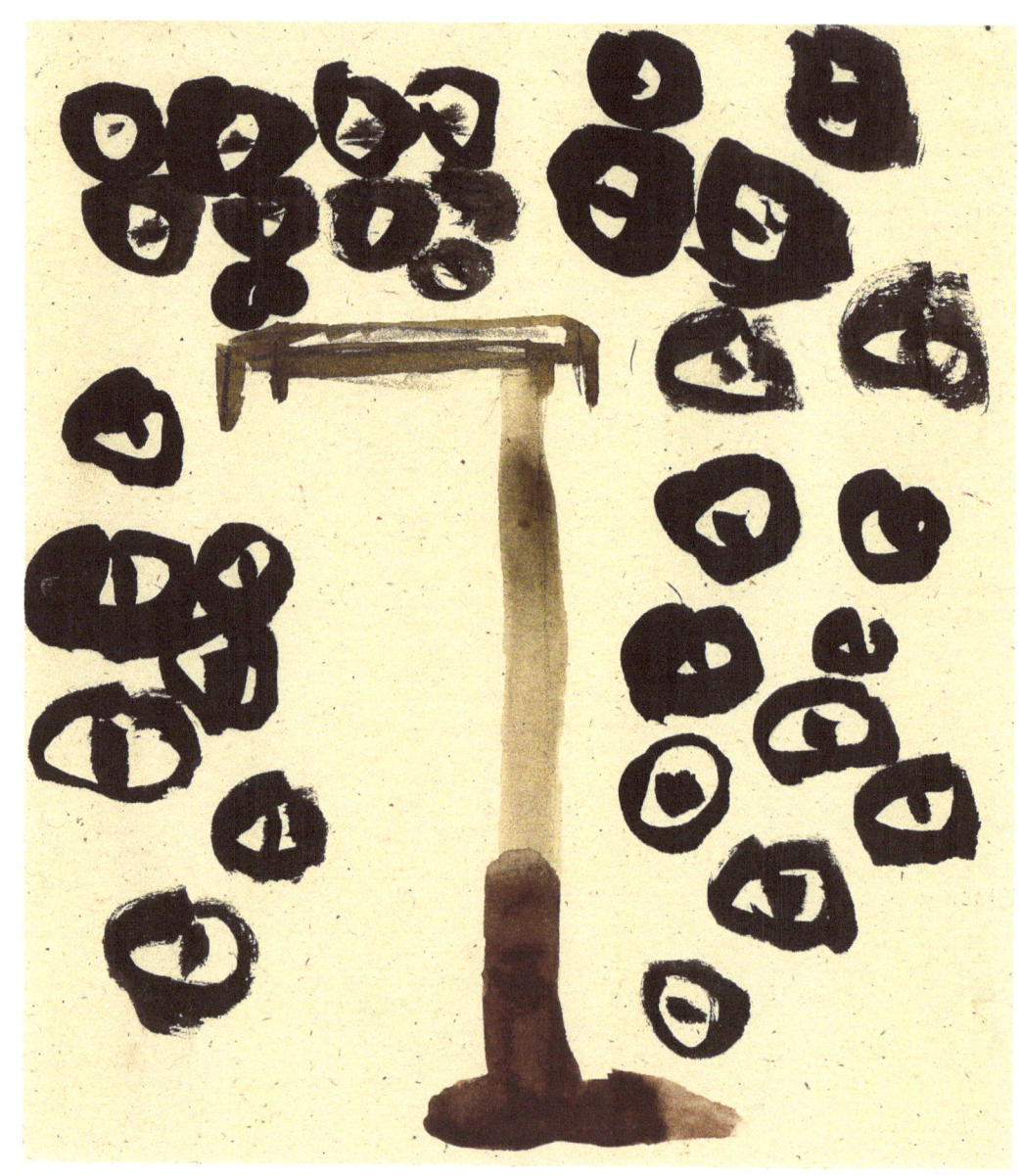

Tuol Sleng Prison
The Khmer Rouge's torture and extermination center.

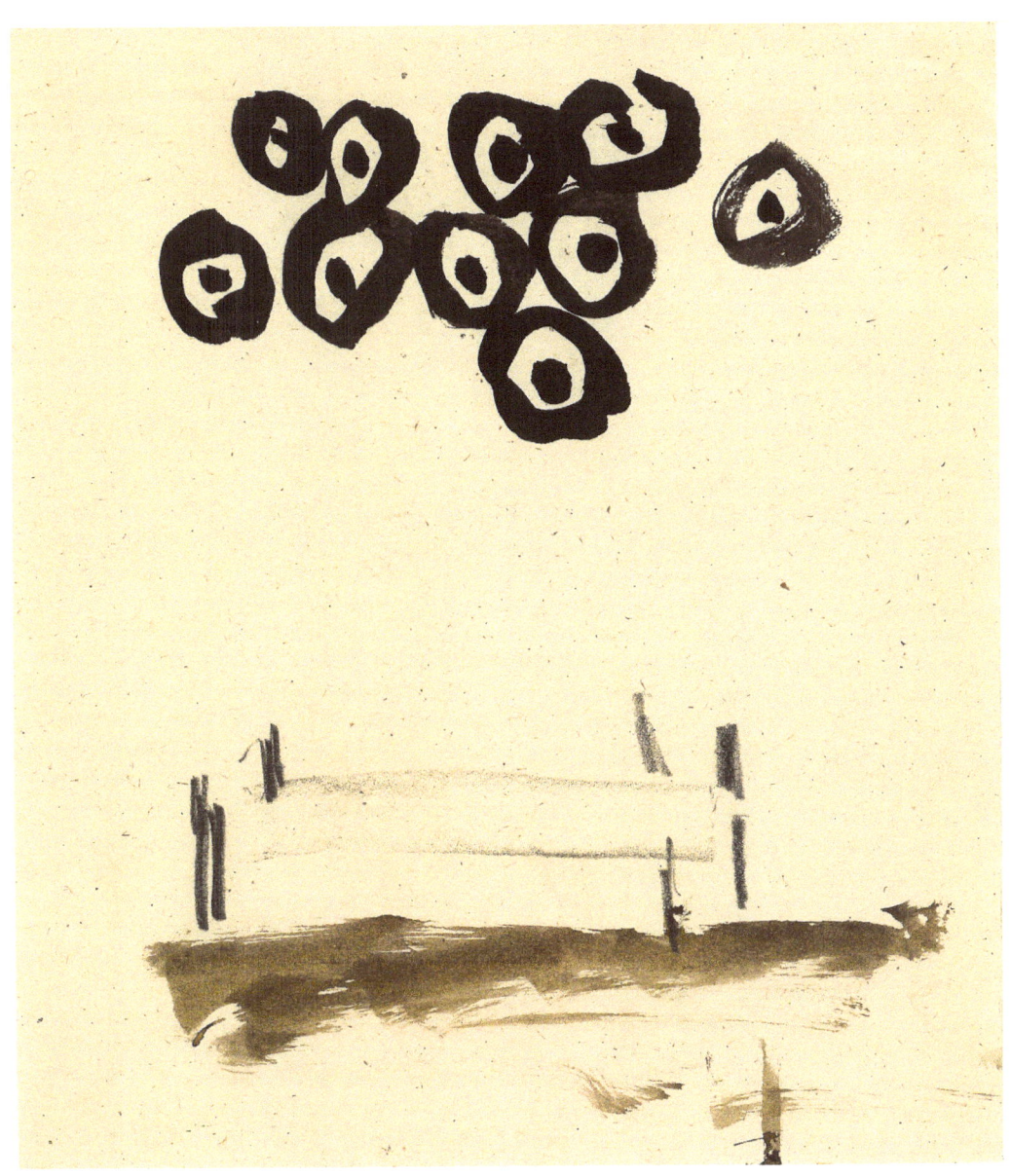

Bearing Witness

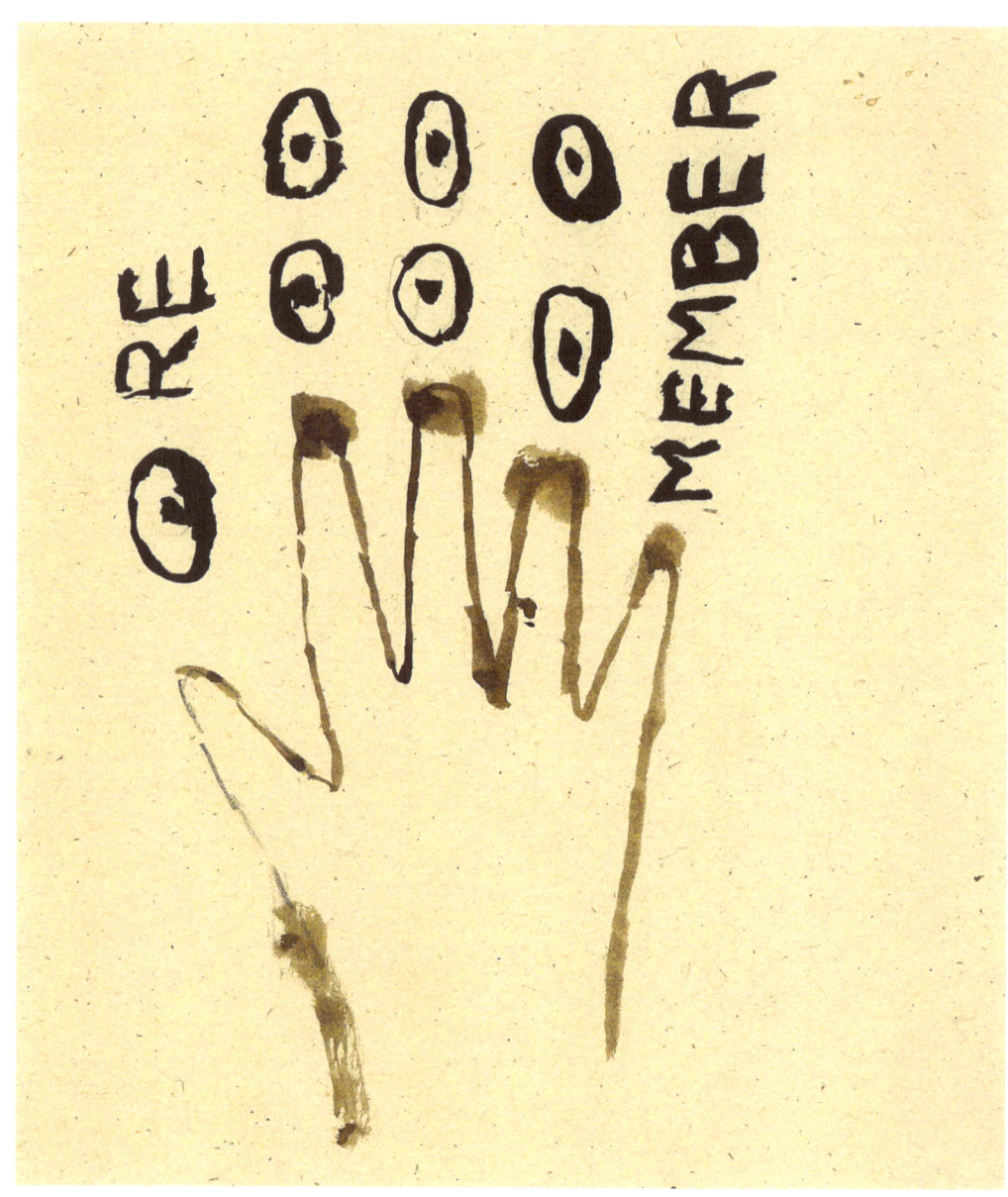

Remember

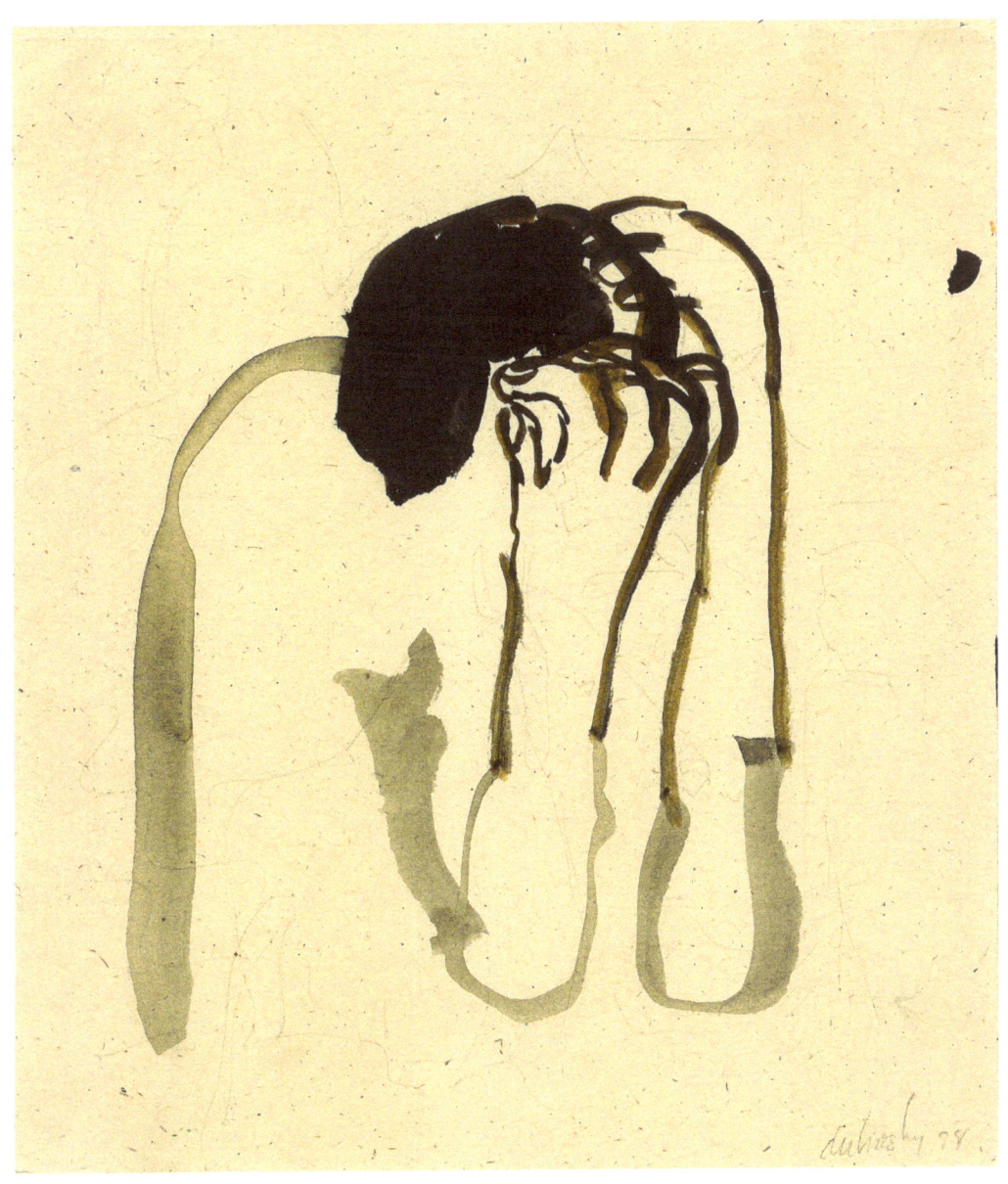

Grief

A LONG TIME OF WAR

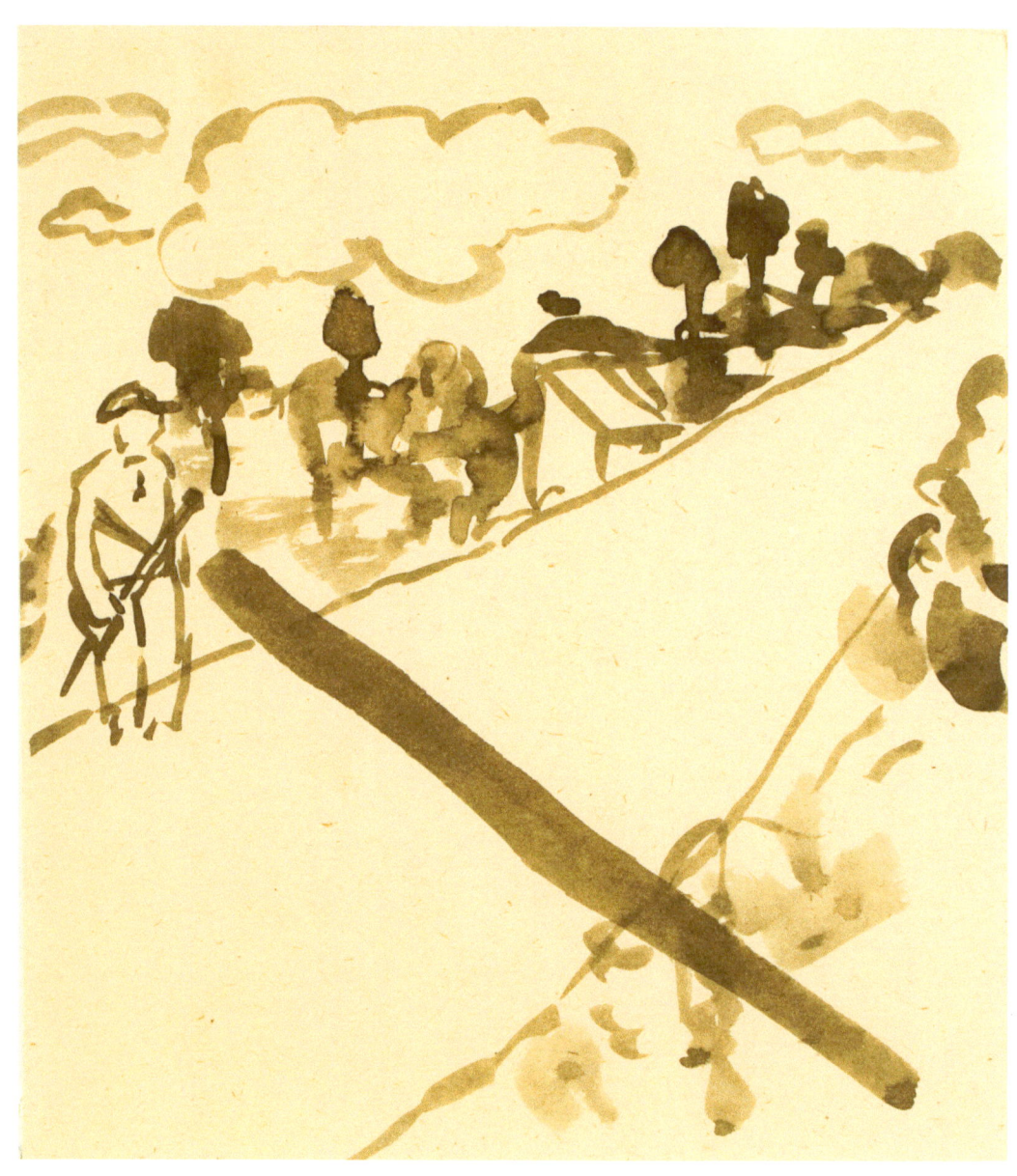

A Roadblock

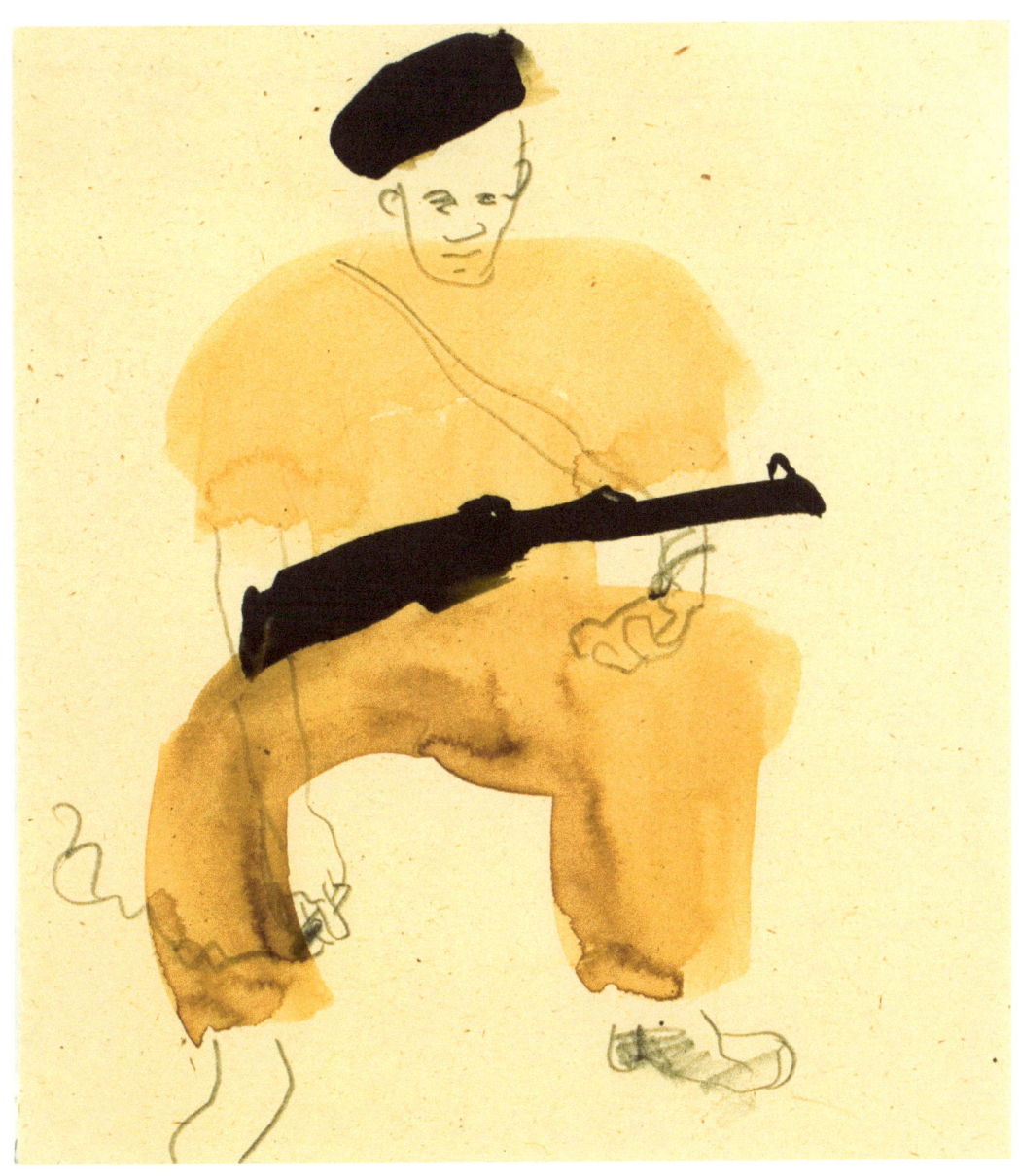

Resting Soldier

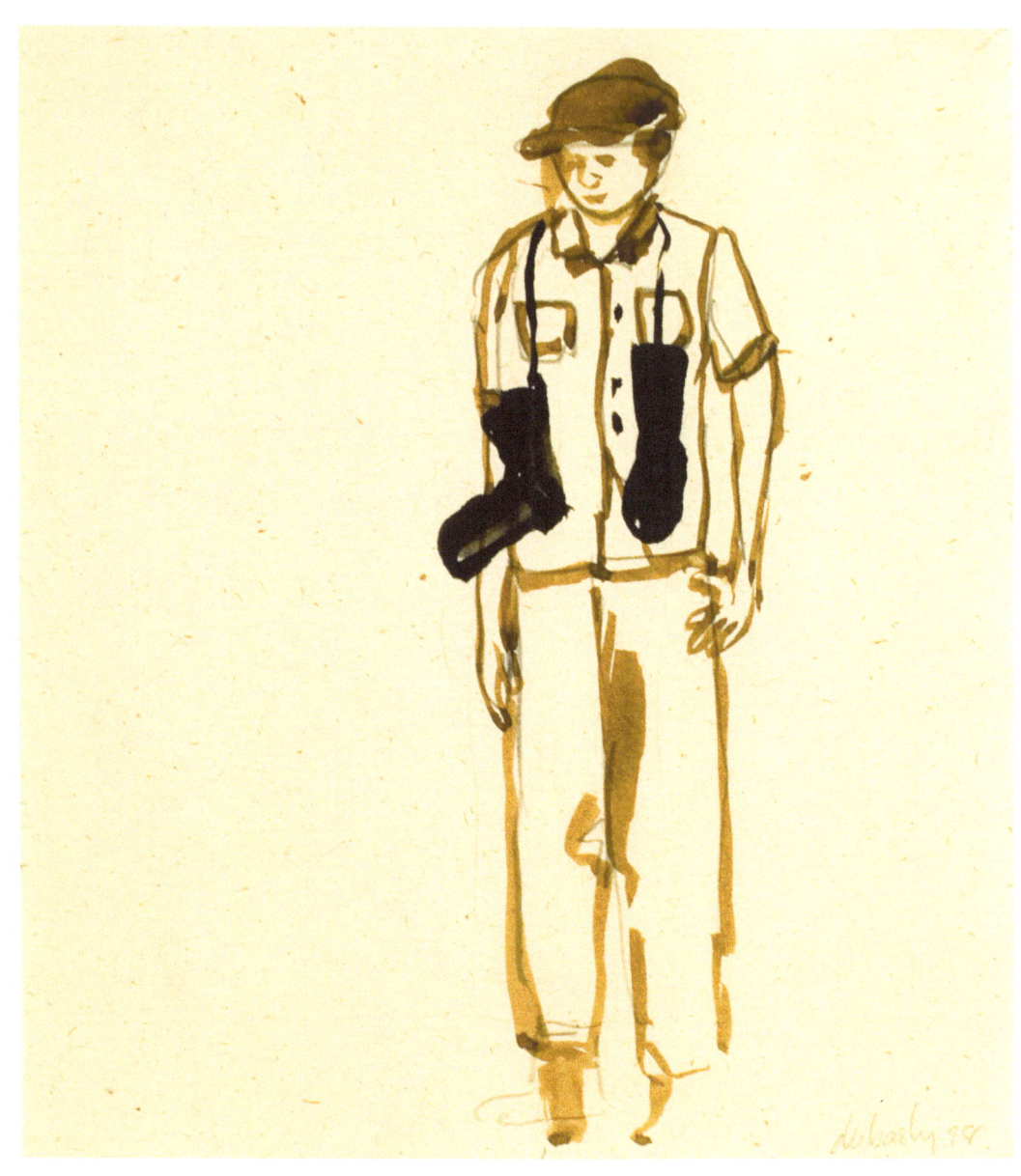

A Barefoot Soldier Carries his Boots

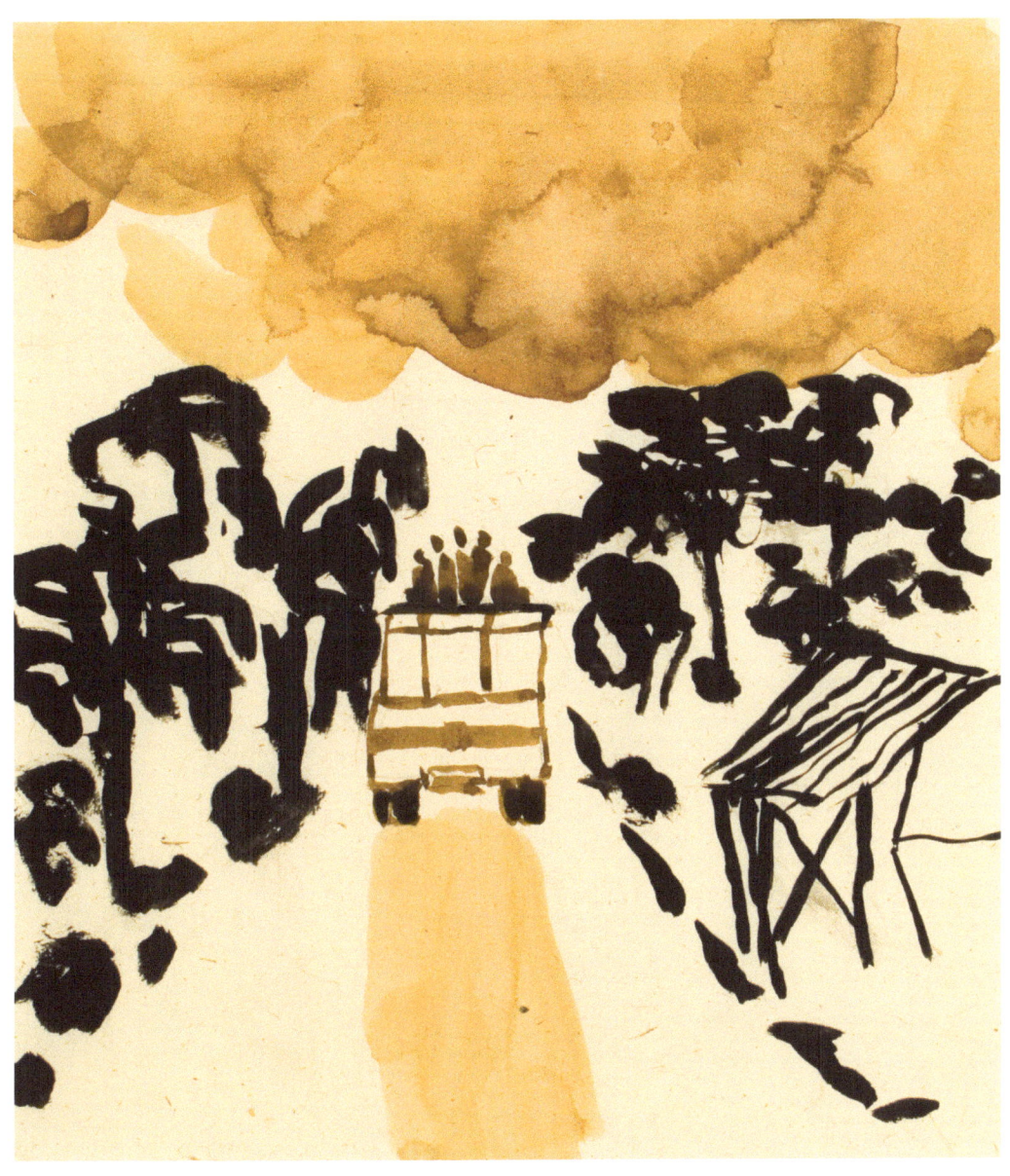

Local Transportation to the Interior
"I didn't want you to worry, so I didn't tell you there are mines on the road."

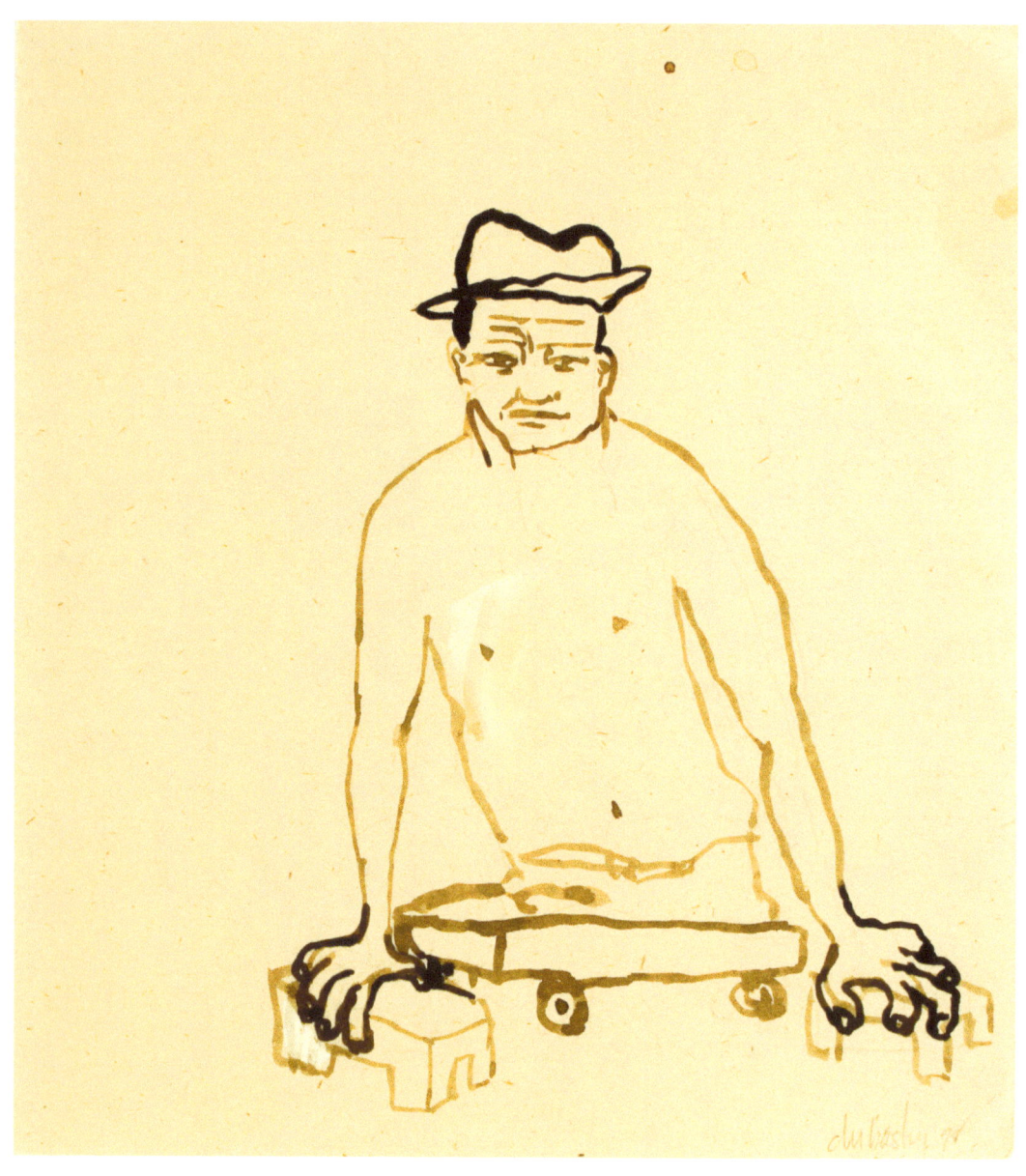

Crossing the Street in Hanoi

WHERE PEOPLE WALK

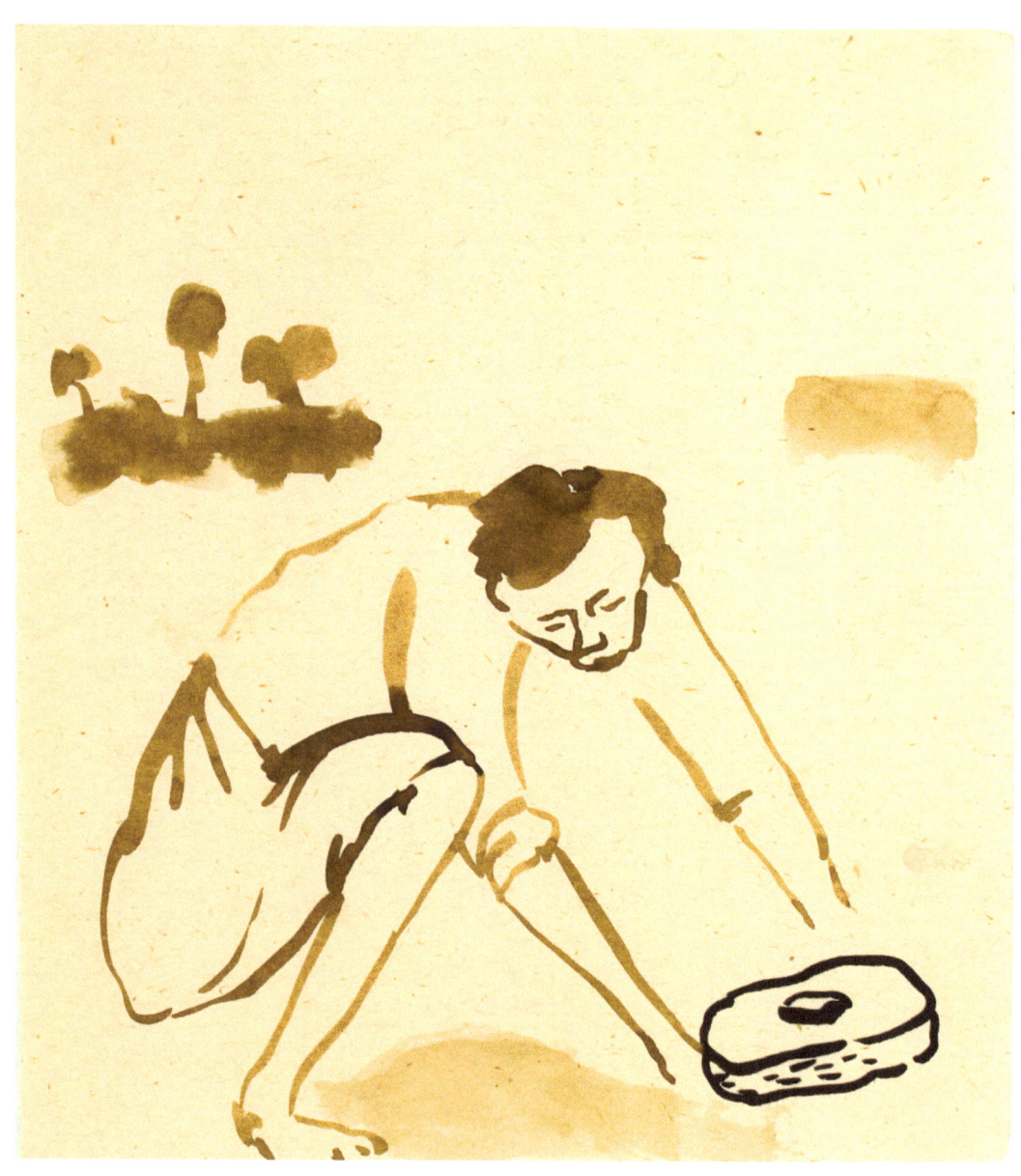

Tragic Harvest: Landmines in his Field

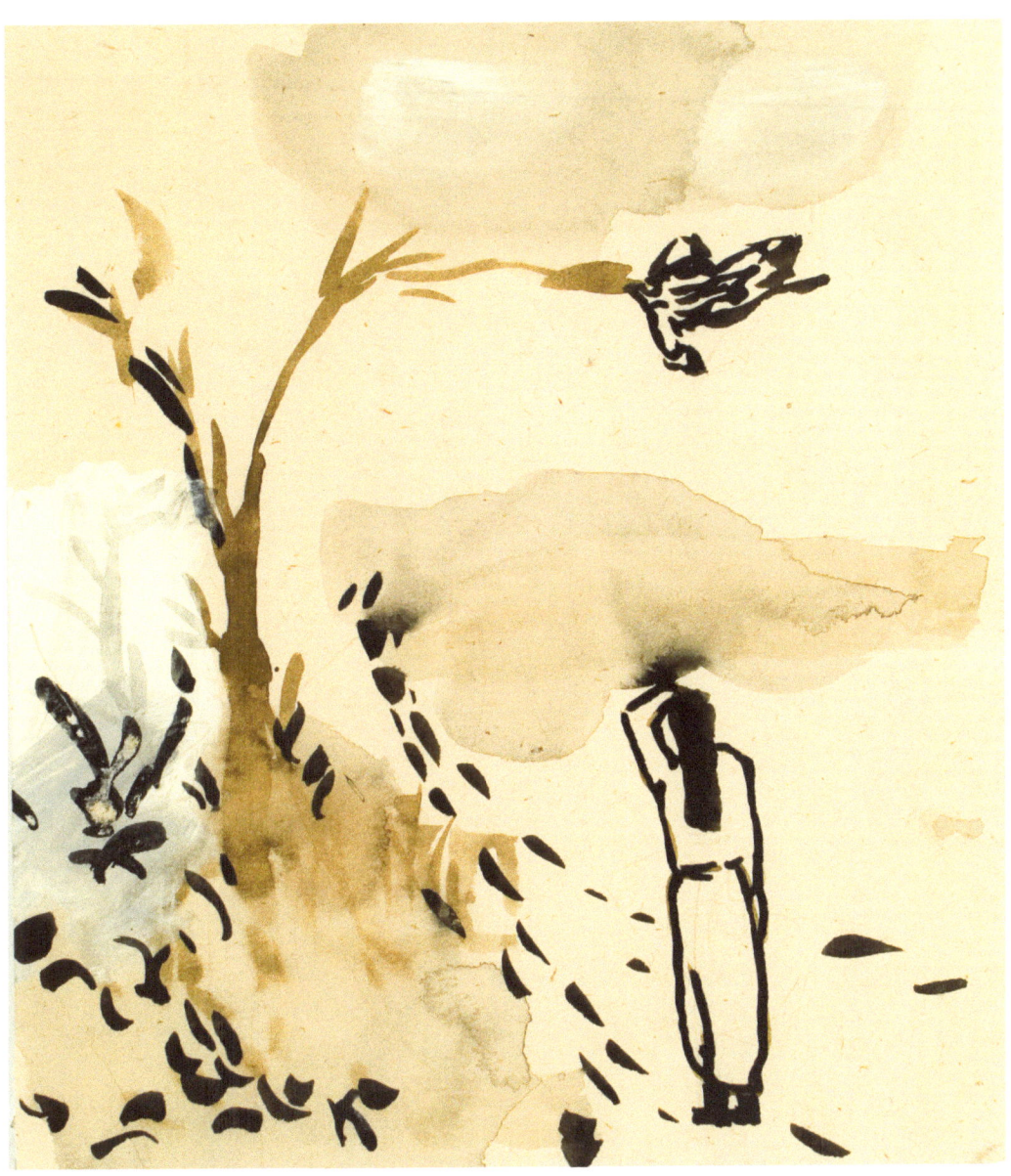

A Shirt on a Branch

One day a man and his wife came home to their village following a trip to the city. The man was very thirsty, so he walked into a field to get a drink of water. He stepped on a POMZ tripwire and was killed instantly. His wife looked for him but his body was nowhere to be found. From the top of some branches his shirt fluttered in the breeze. — *from the Cambodian Mines Action Center (CMAC)*

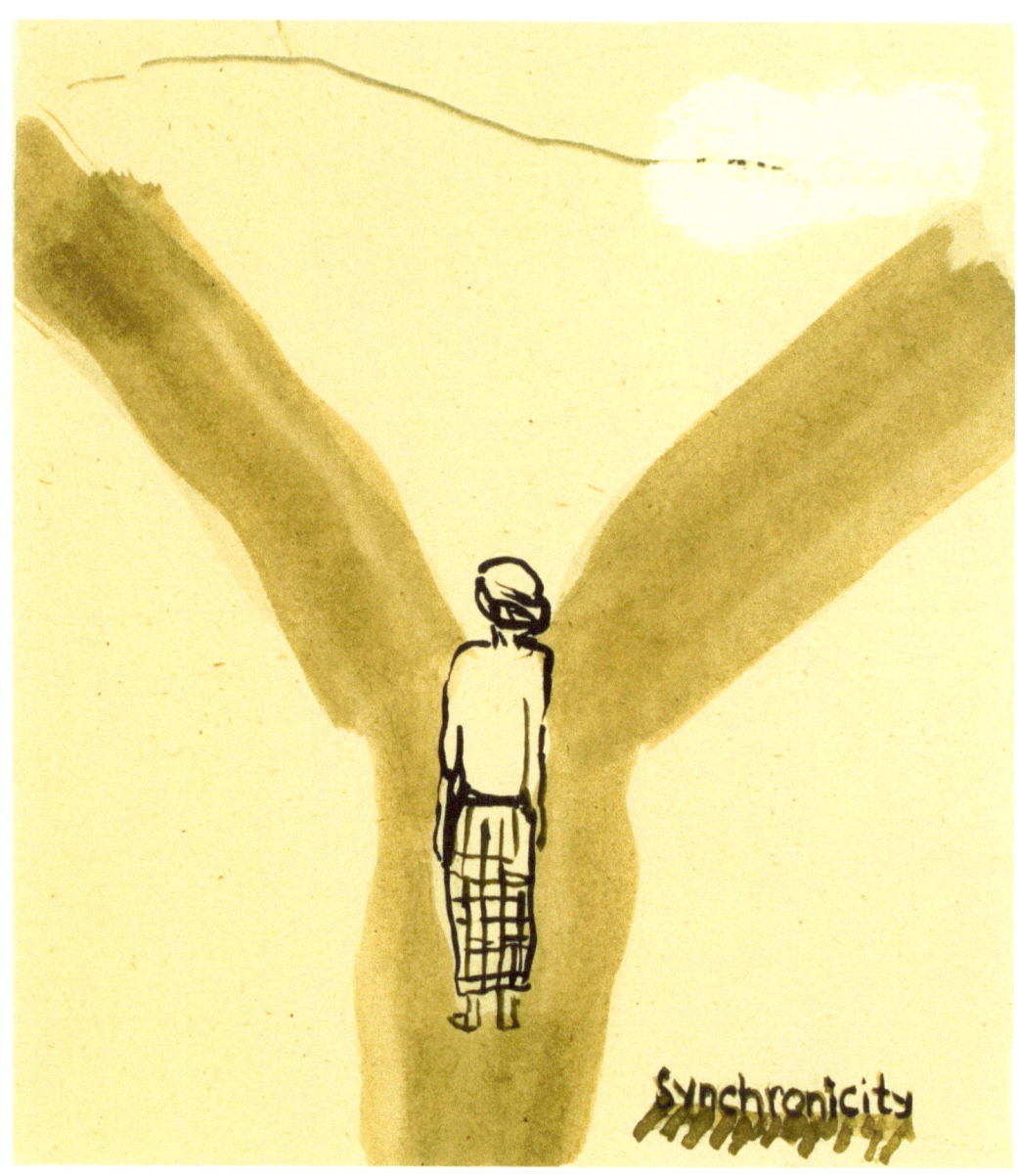

Fate or Chance

To avoid mines when traveling in an unknown area, stay on well used roads or paths, walk in the center of the safe path as the edges may be mined. Do not travel before sunrise or after sunset, as soldiers are known to lay mines at night and remove them in the morning. — from the Cambodian Mines Action Center (CMAC)

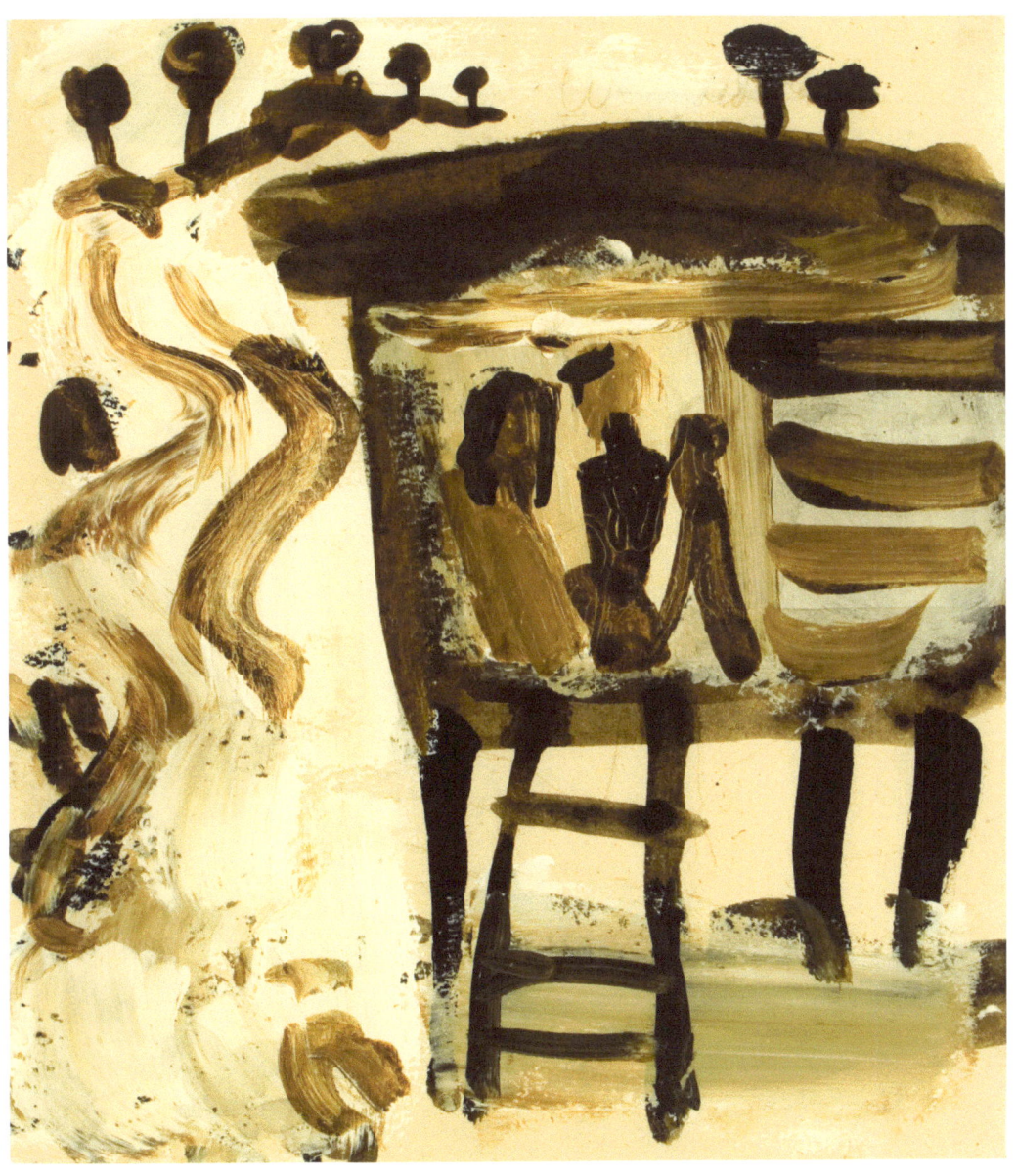

Internally Displaced Persons Site

At an Internally Displaced Persons Site (IDP), families displaced by landmines and civil war live in small, crowded houses. Not far from here, near Prasat, are the Khmer Rouge regional headquarters.

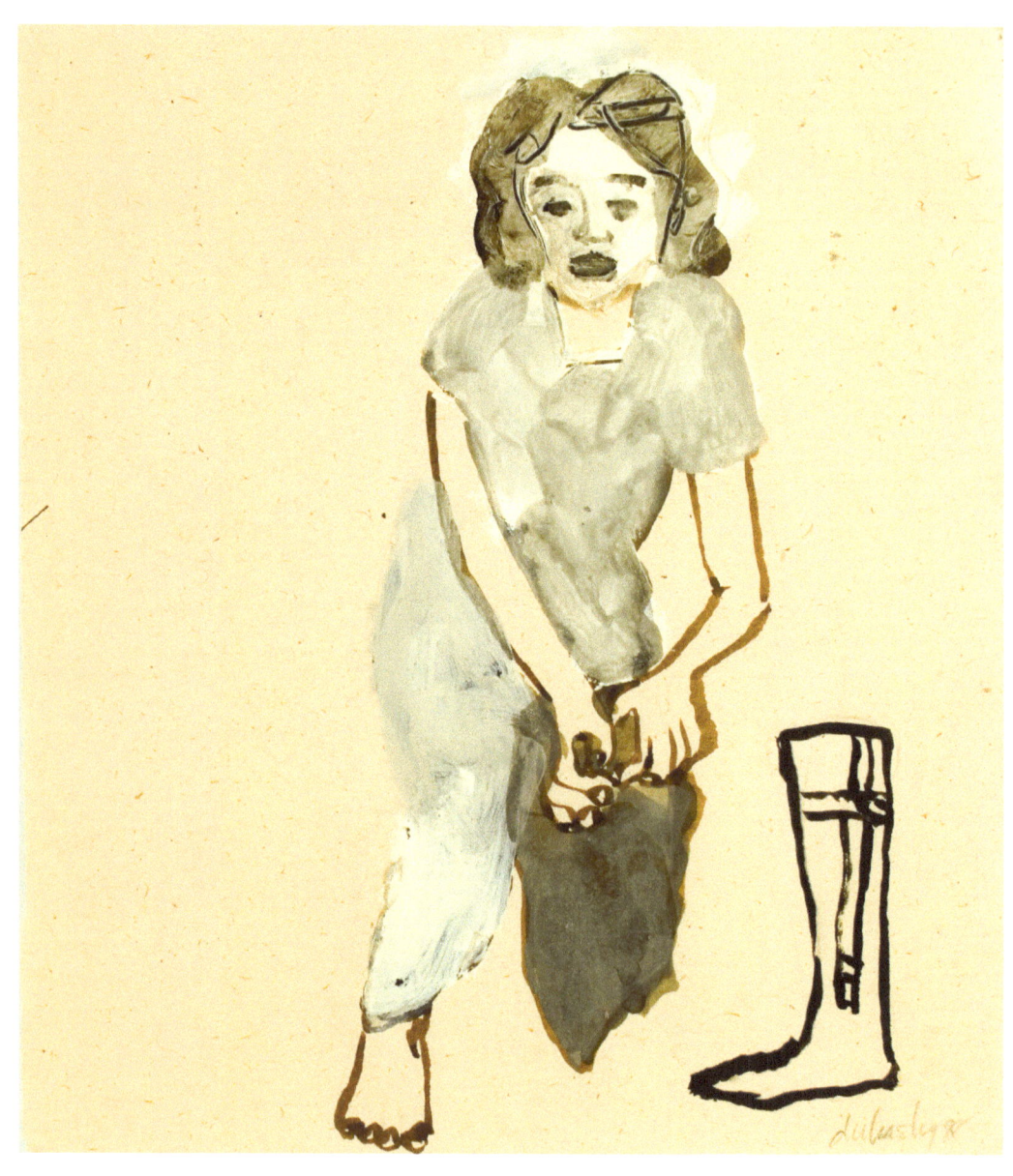

Maline's Mother Worried About Her
She worried that the road might not be safe. It wasn't landmines that worried her;
she worried about soldiers on the road.

IN THE TEMPLE OF OUR HEARTS

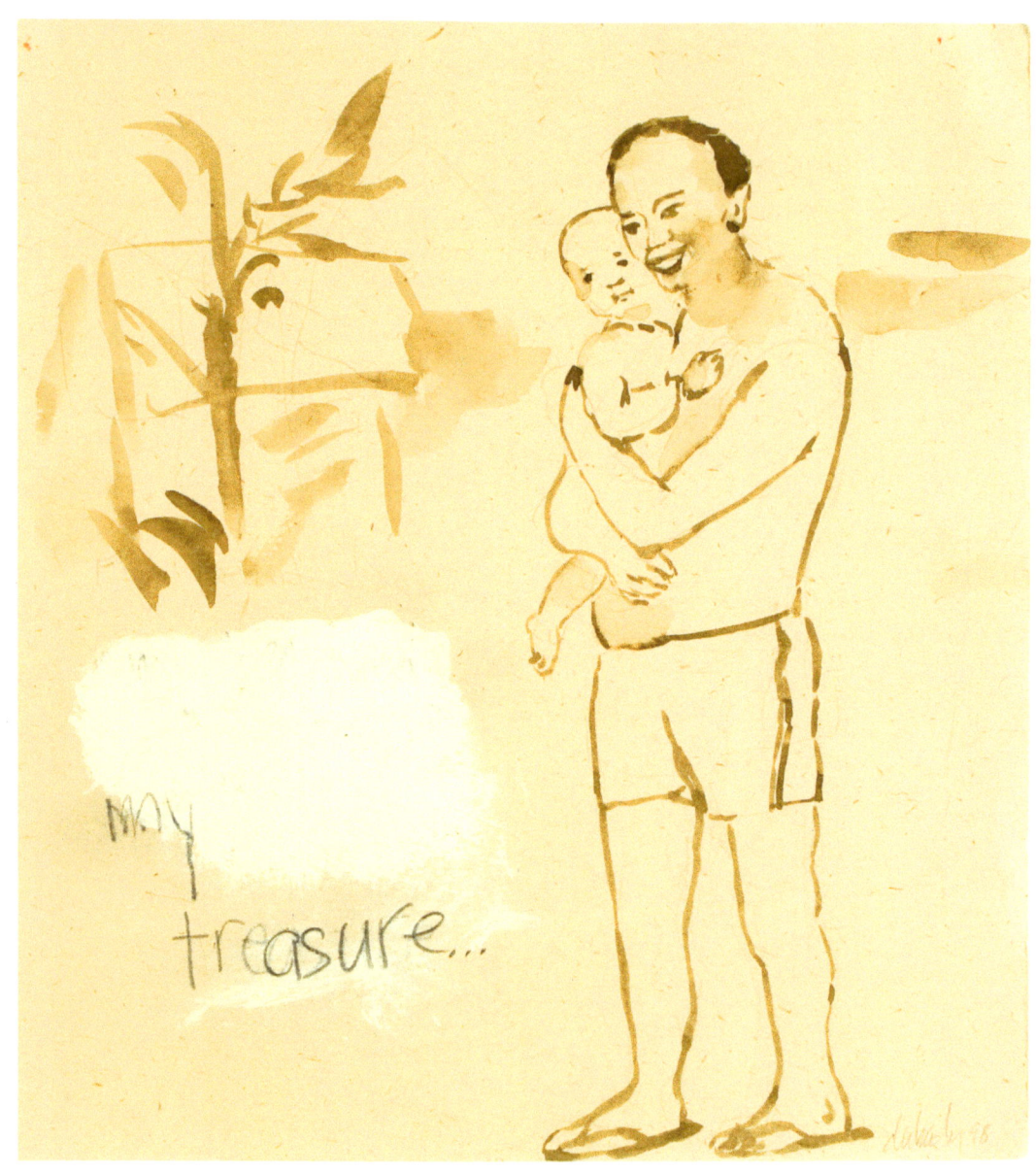

His Treasure

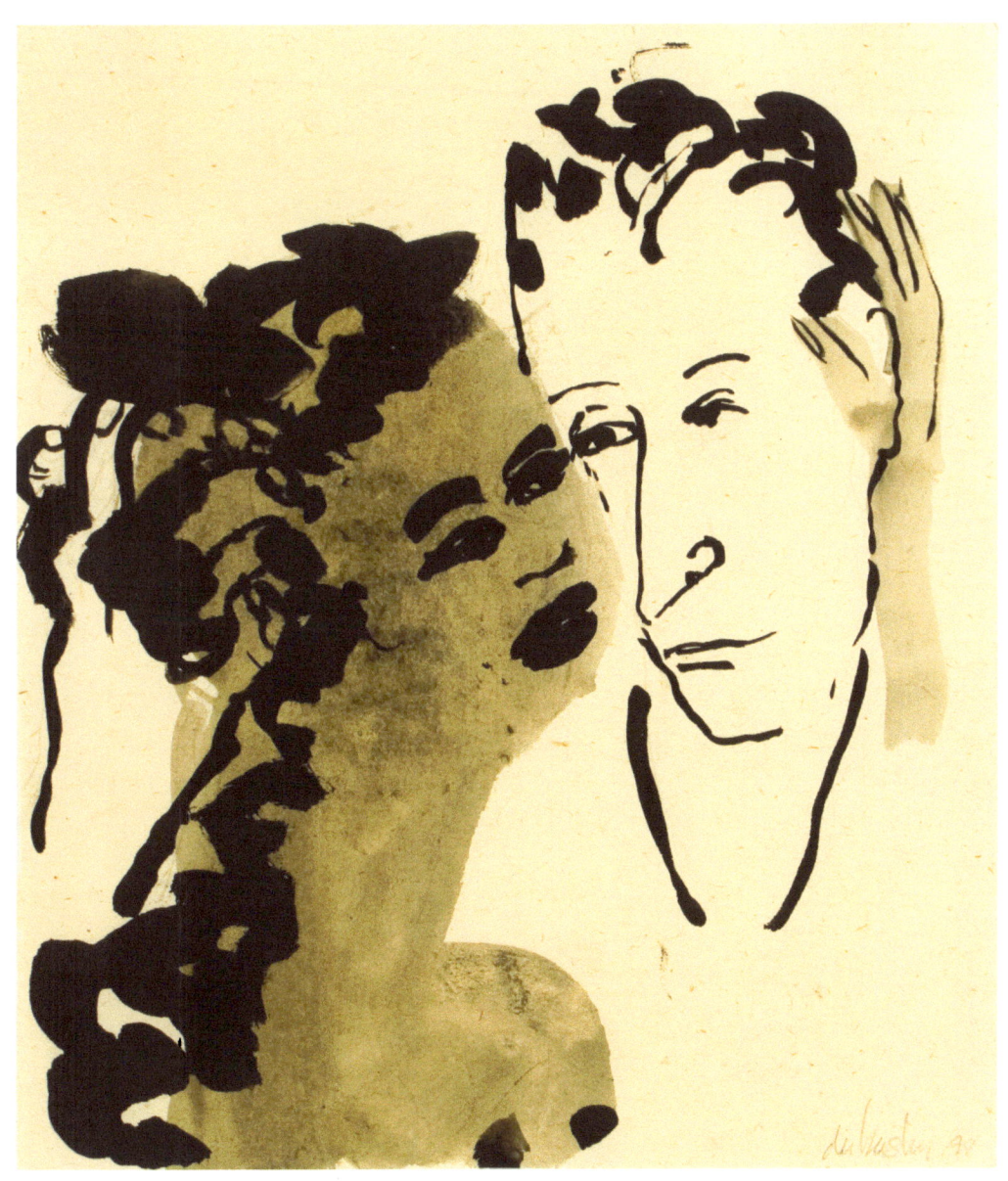

Lovers

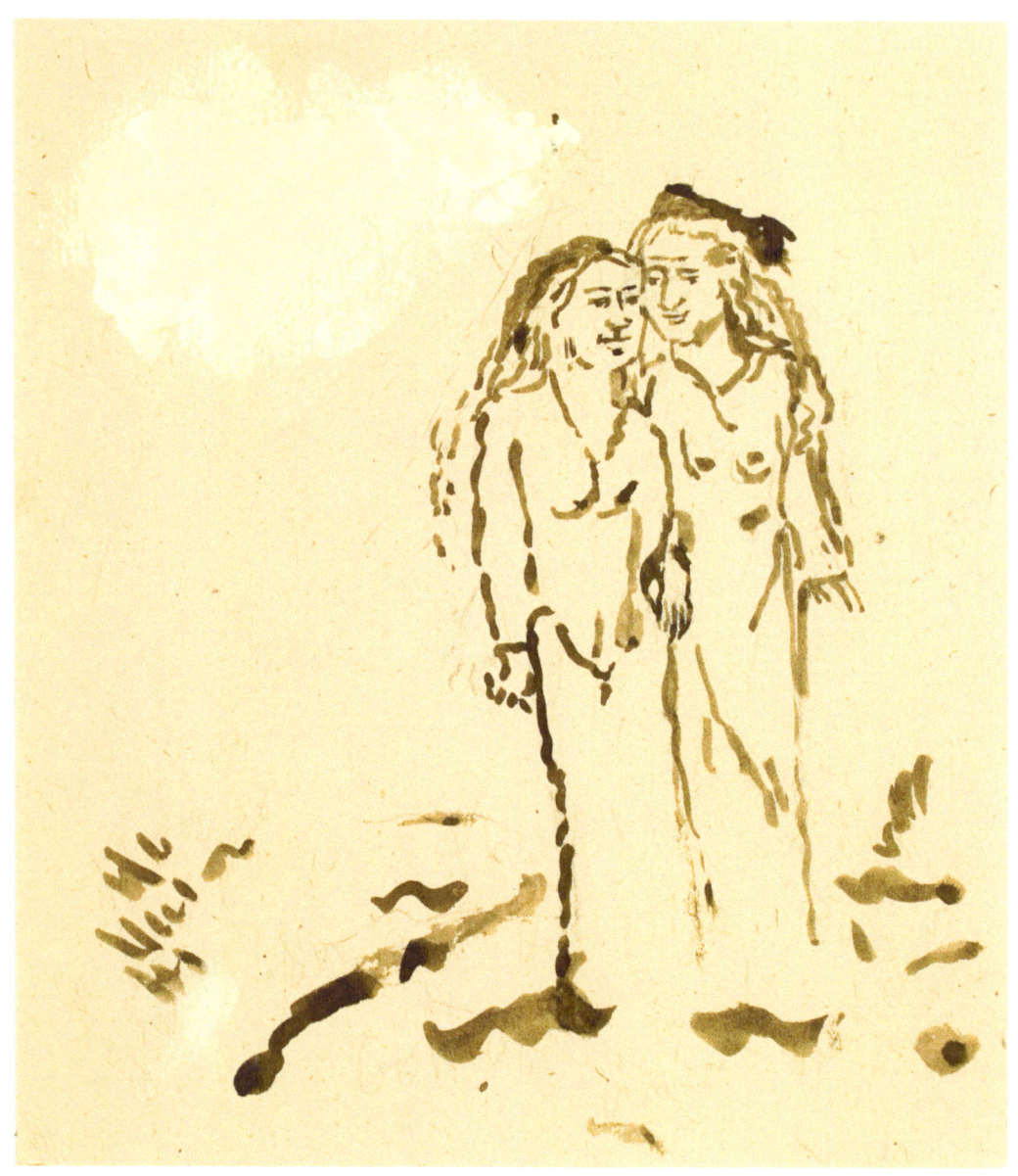

The Wedding of Kep Sokha and Soth Ek

More than 250 friends and relatives attended the wedding of Kep Sokha and Soth Ek. Sok Ek had suffered from a lingering illness and came to Sokha for treatment. Sokha cured her and then courted her. The happy couple have become local celebrities.

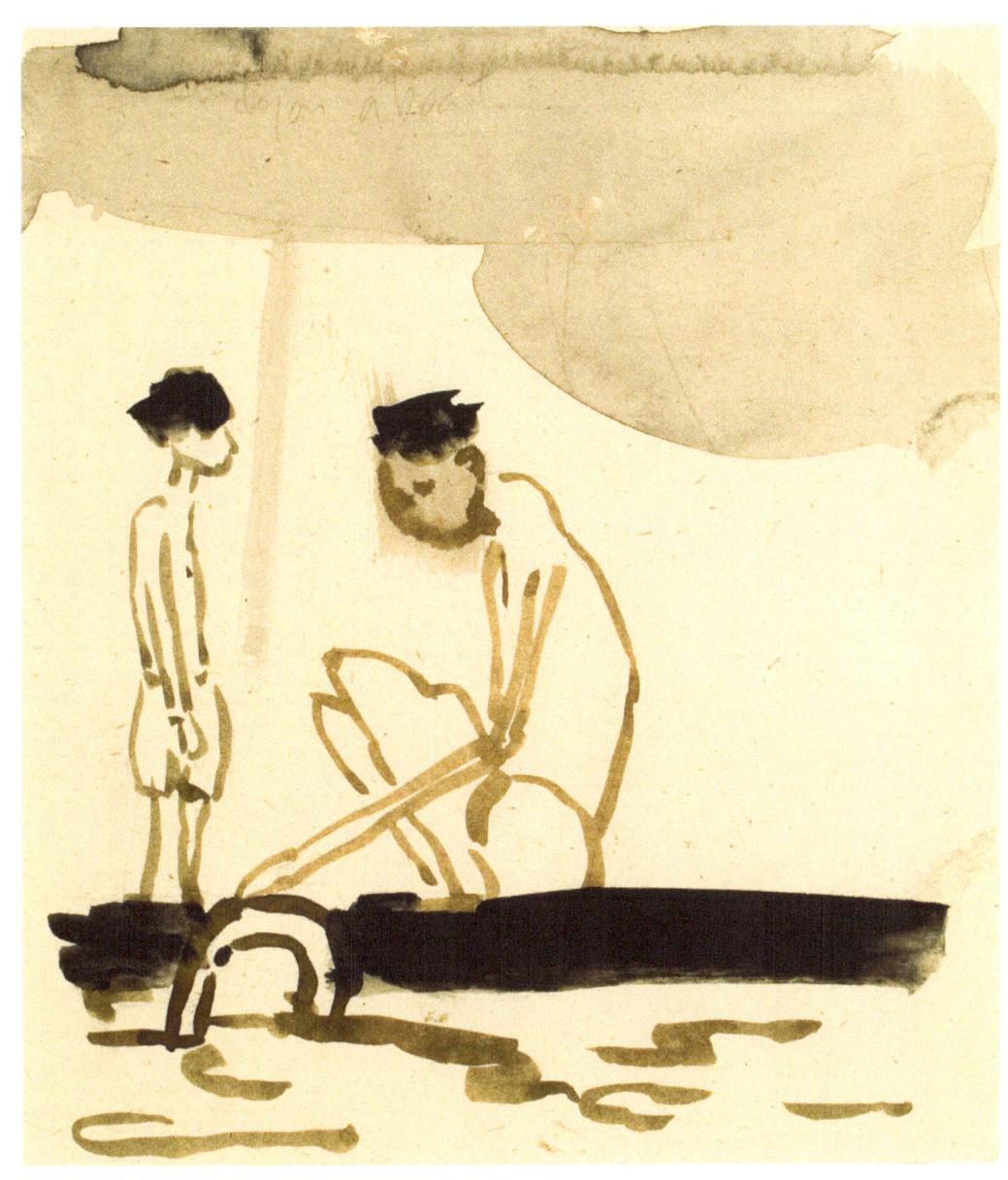

Washing Dishes in the Mekong River

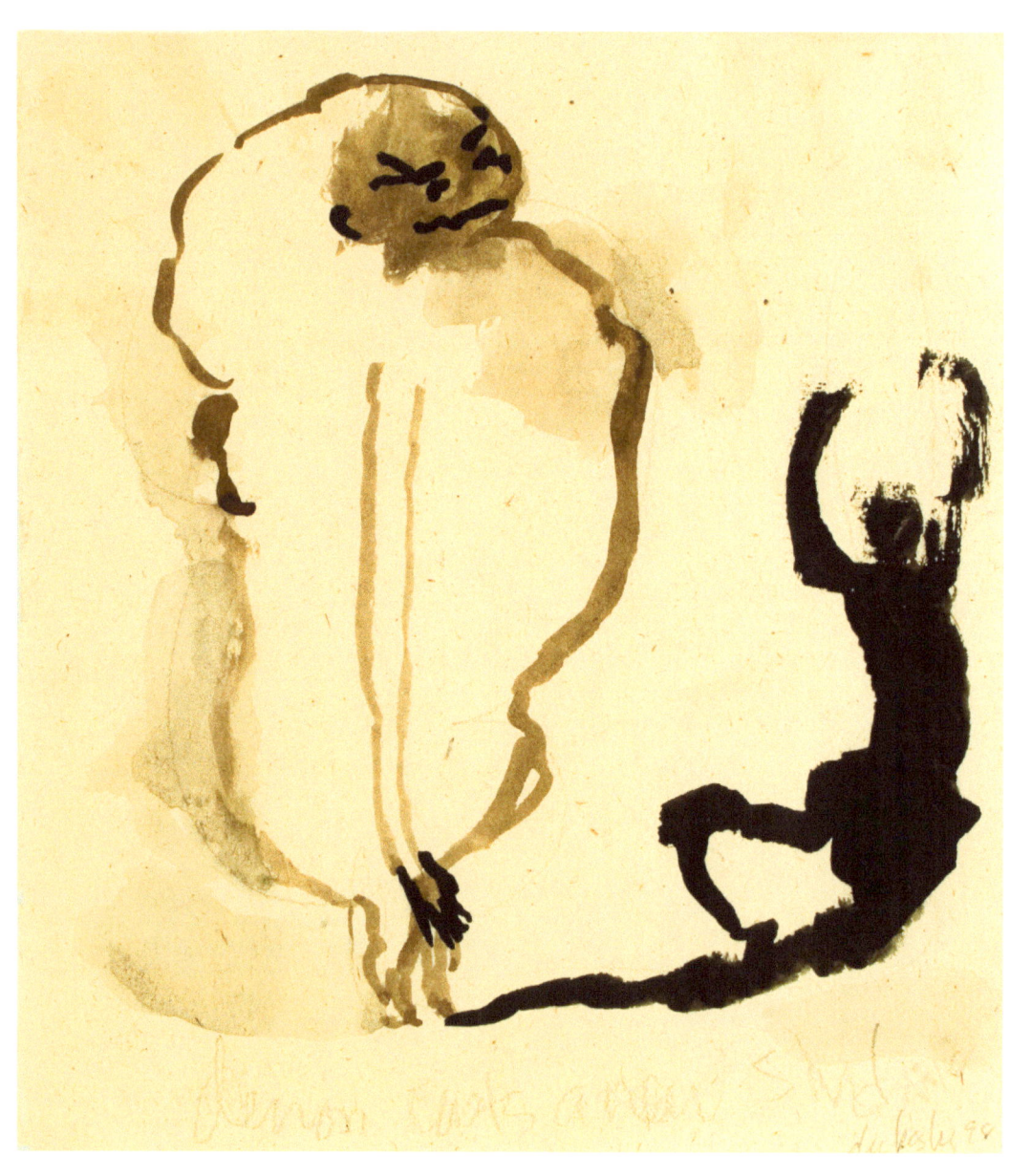

The Beast Was Once a Magical Child

AN UNCERTAIN FUTURE

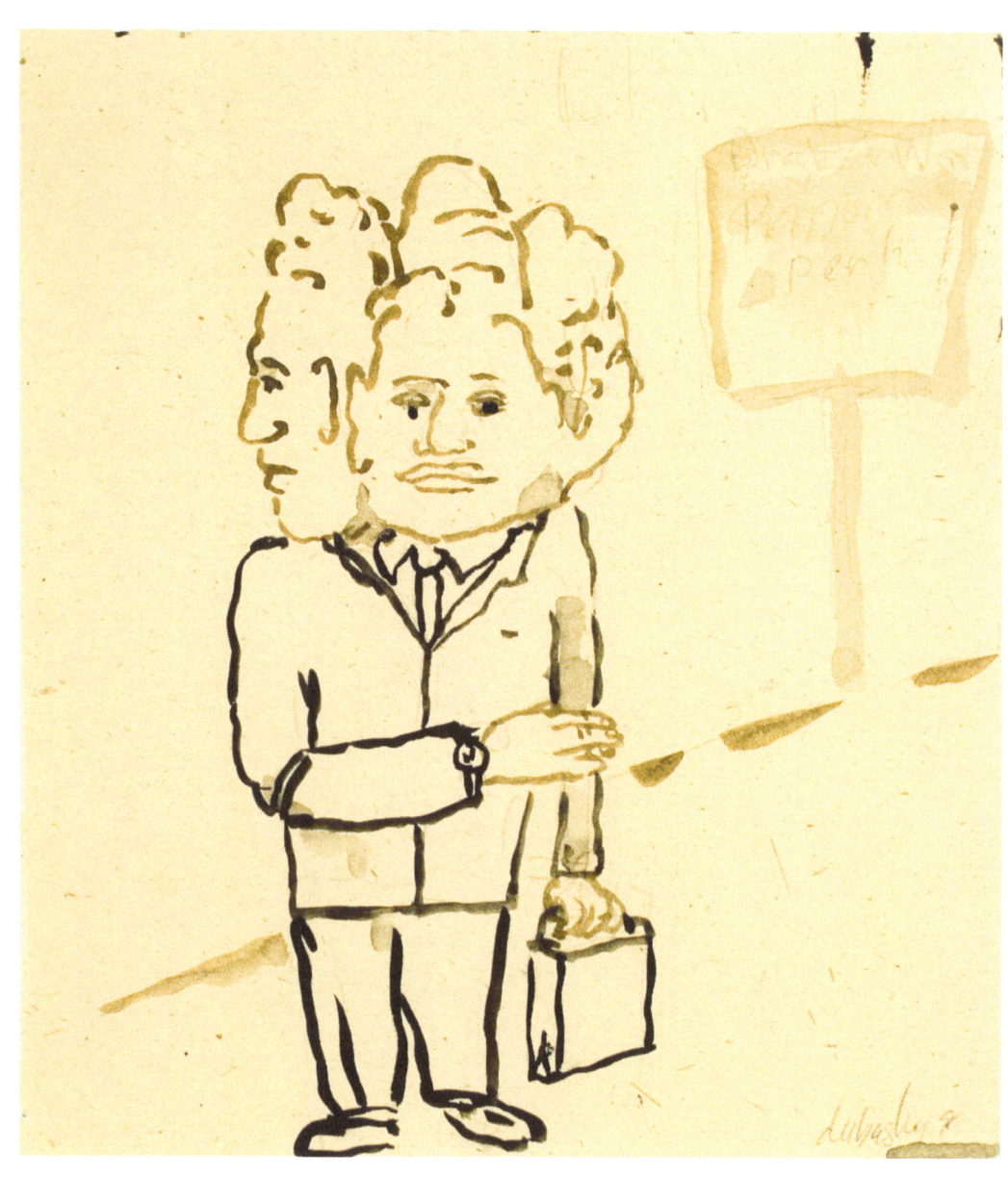

Cambodia Prepares for National Elections

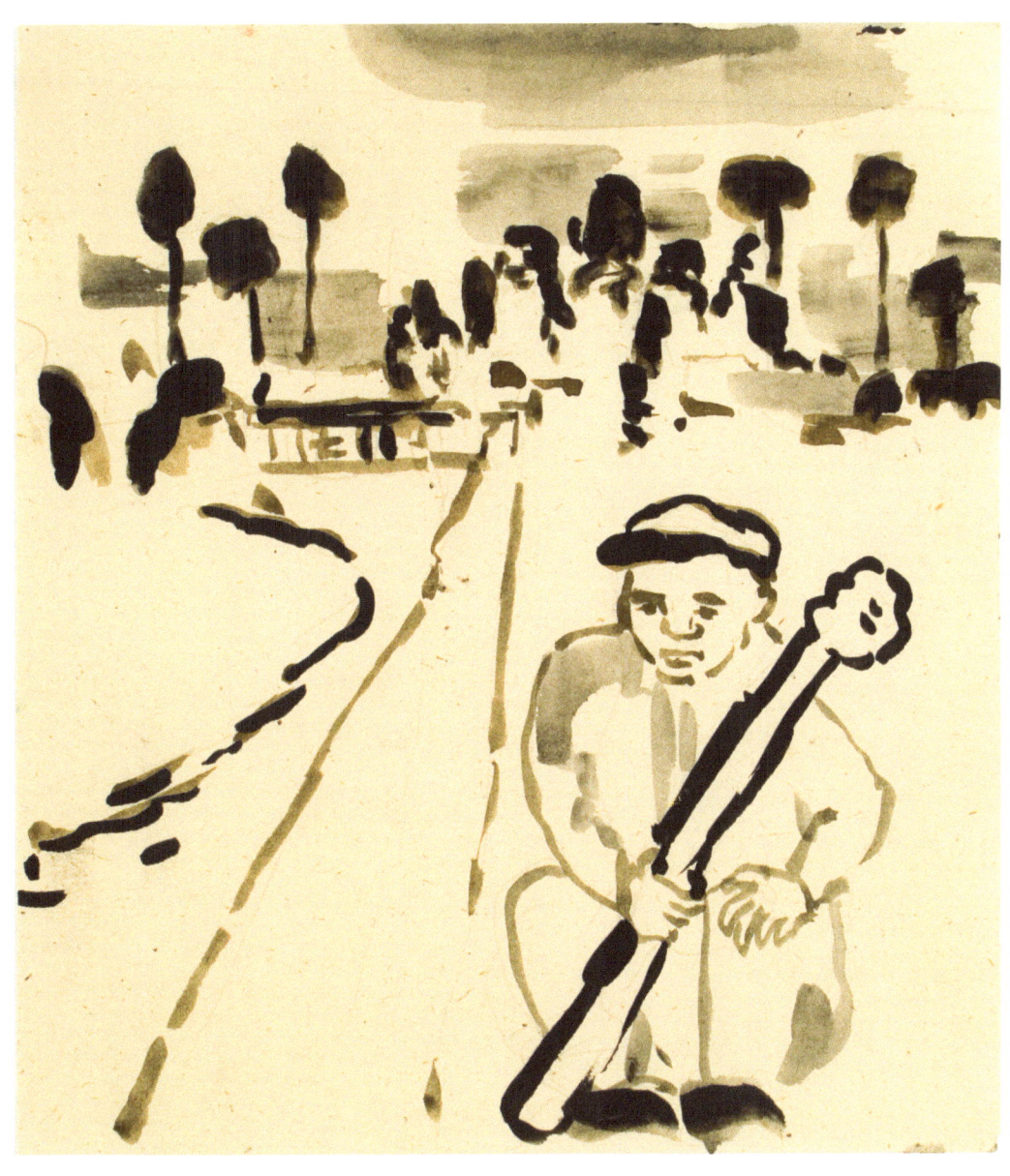

Night Watch at Angkor Wat
A soldier with a grenade gun takes the night watch at Angkor Wat.

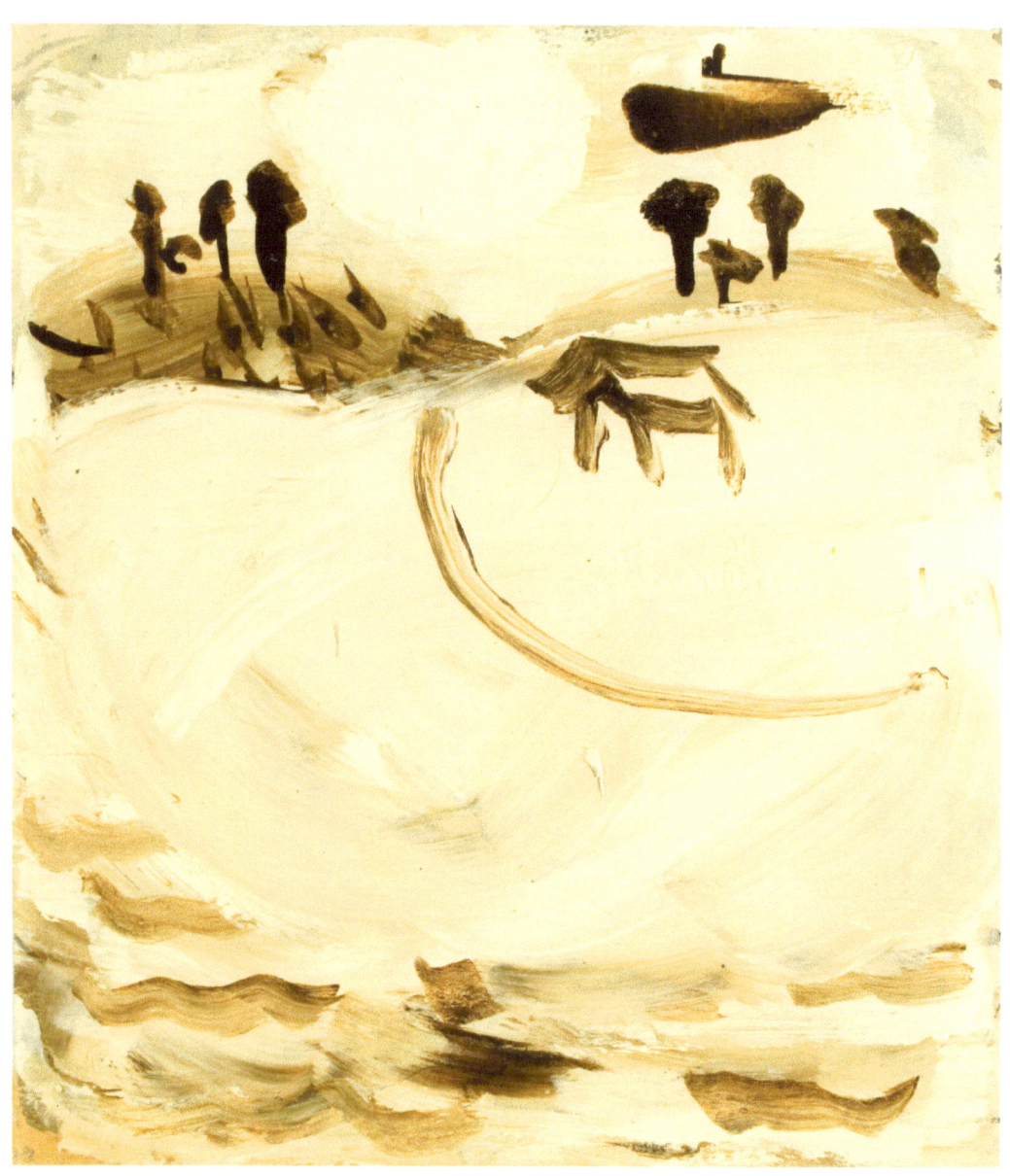

Toxic Waste in Sihanoukeville

Shipping vessels from Taiwan dumped toxic waste in plastic bags on this beautiful beach in Sihanoukeville. The local people took the plastic bags to store rice and unraveled the strands of plastic to mend the oxen's yokes. The children played in the white powder.

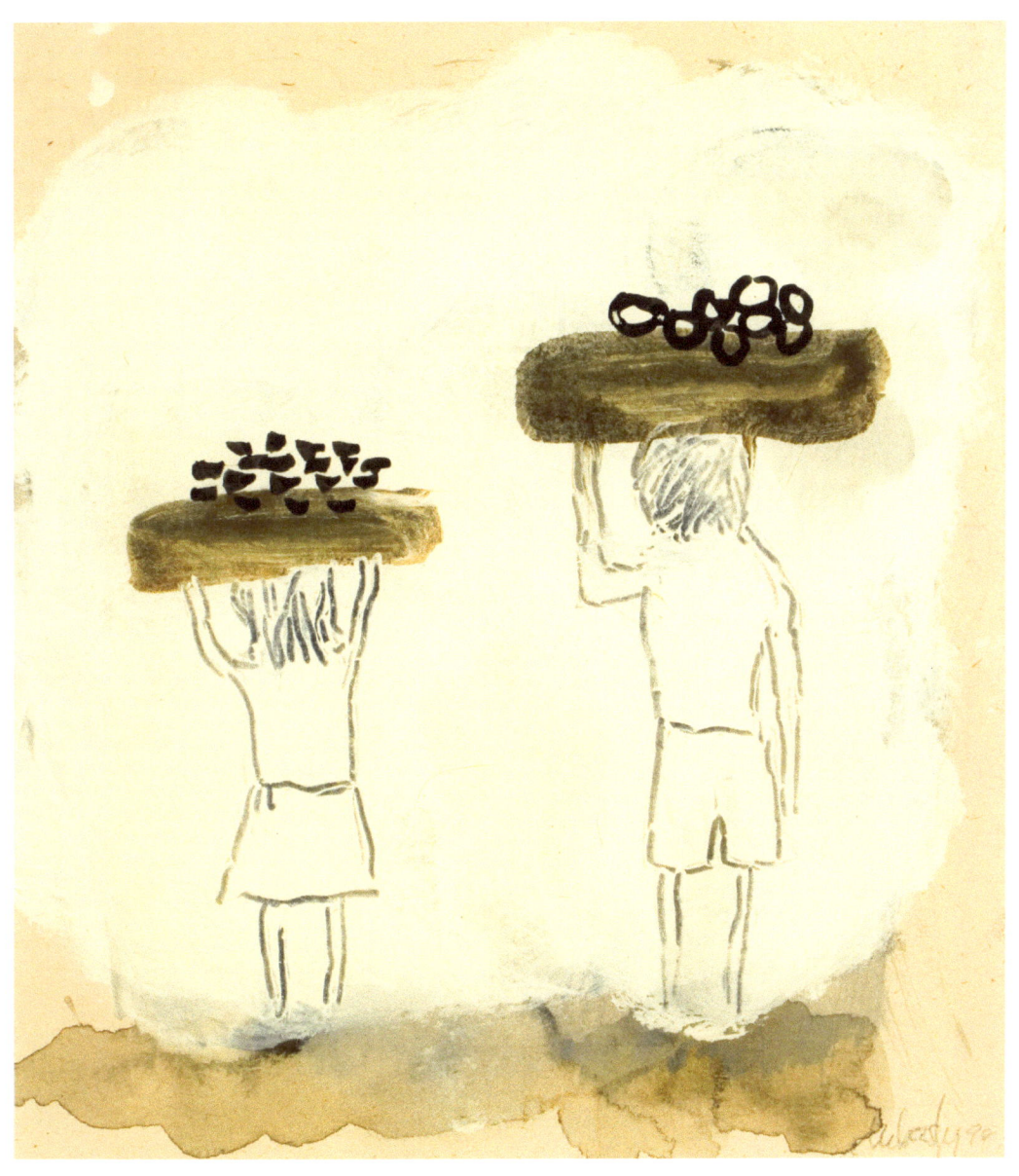

Children Selling Snacks

Children sell spider kabobs, cigarettes and drinks from baskets as wide as old moons.

STORIES AND TEACHINGS
FOR THE JOURNEY

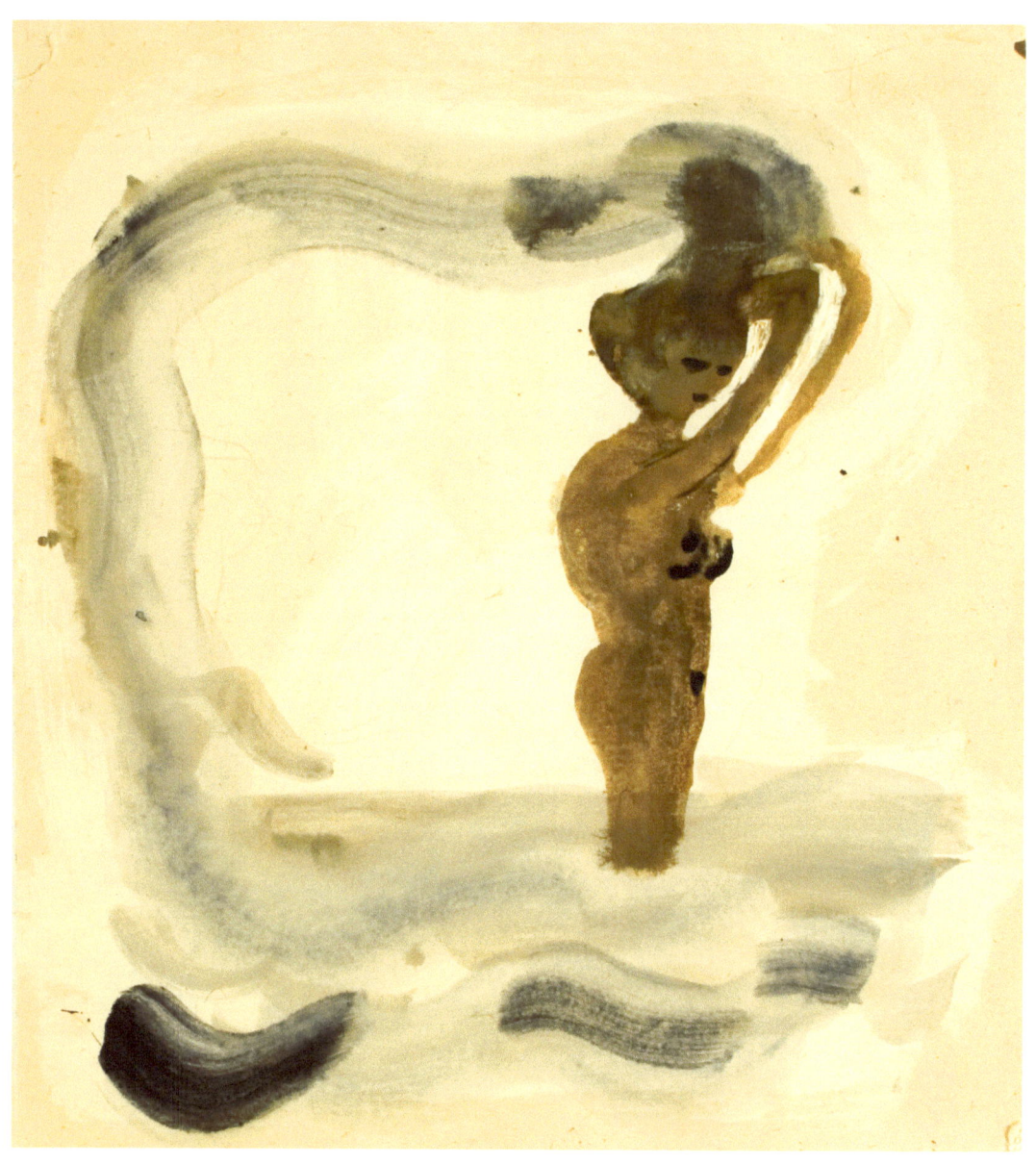

Saraswati Washes her Hair in the Mekong River (after a Khmer bronze)

At the beginning of time, Saraswati, the goddess of literature, music and the arts, washed her hair in the Mekong River. Iridescent fish, white cattle egrets, green and copper frogs and serpents slid from her hair. The animals were her gift to the Cambodian people so they could have abundance for all their days.

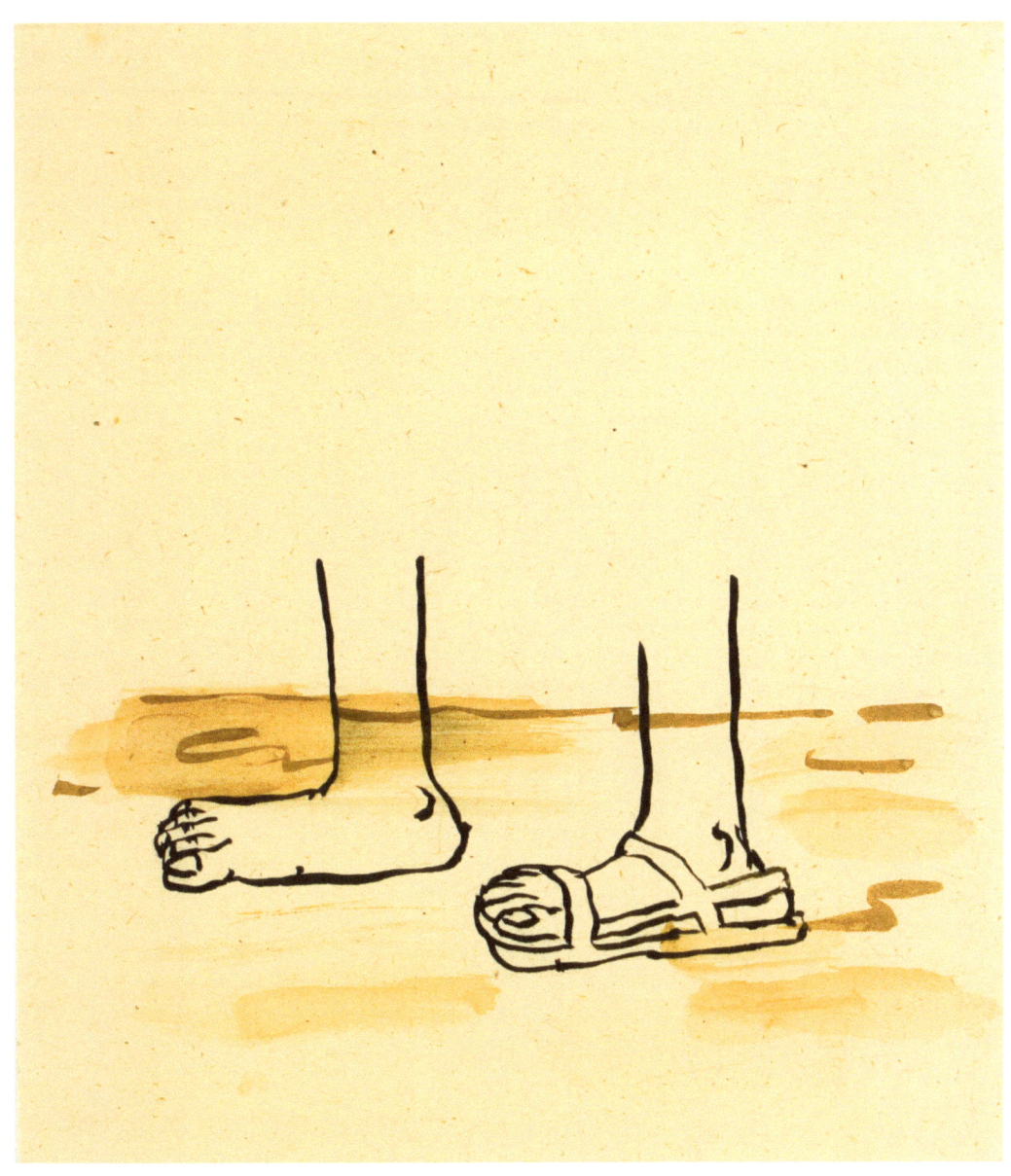

Crossing the Water (Coming Home)

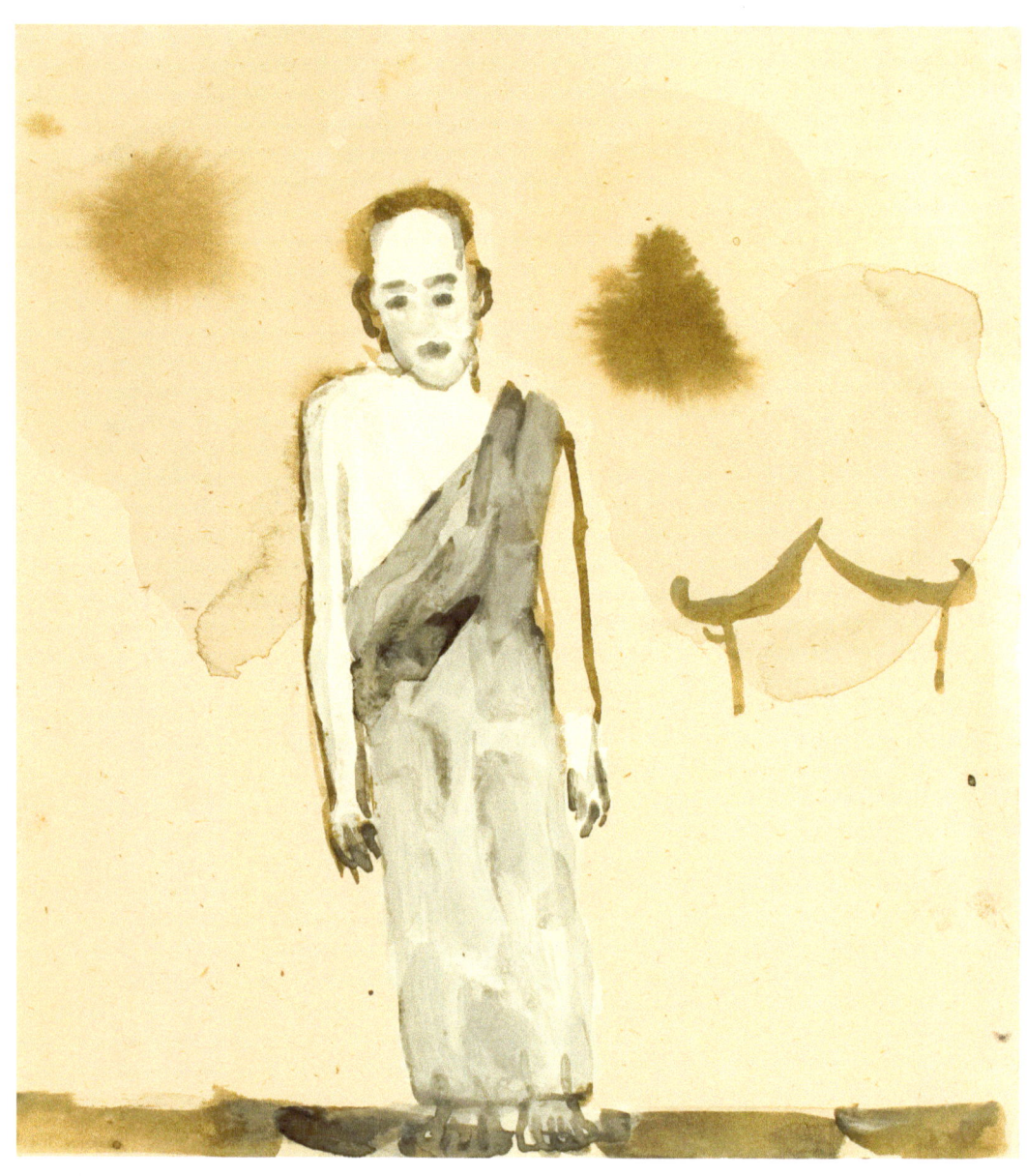

A Peace Monk

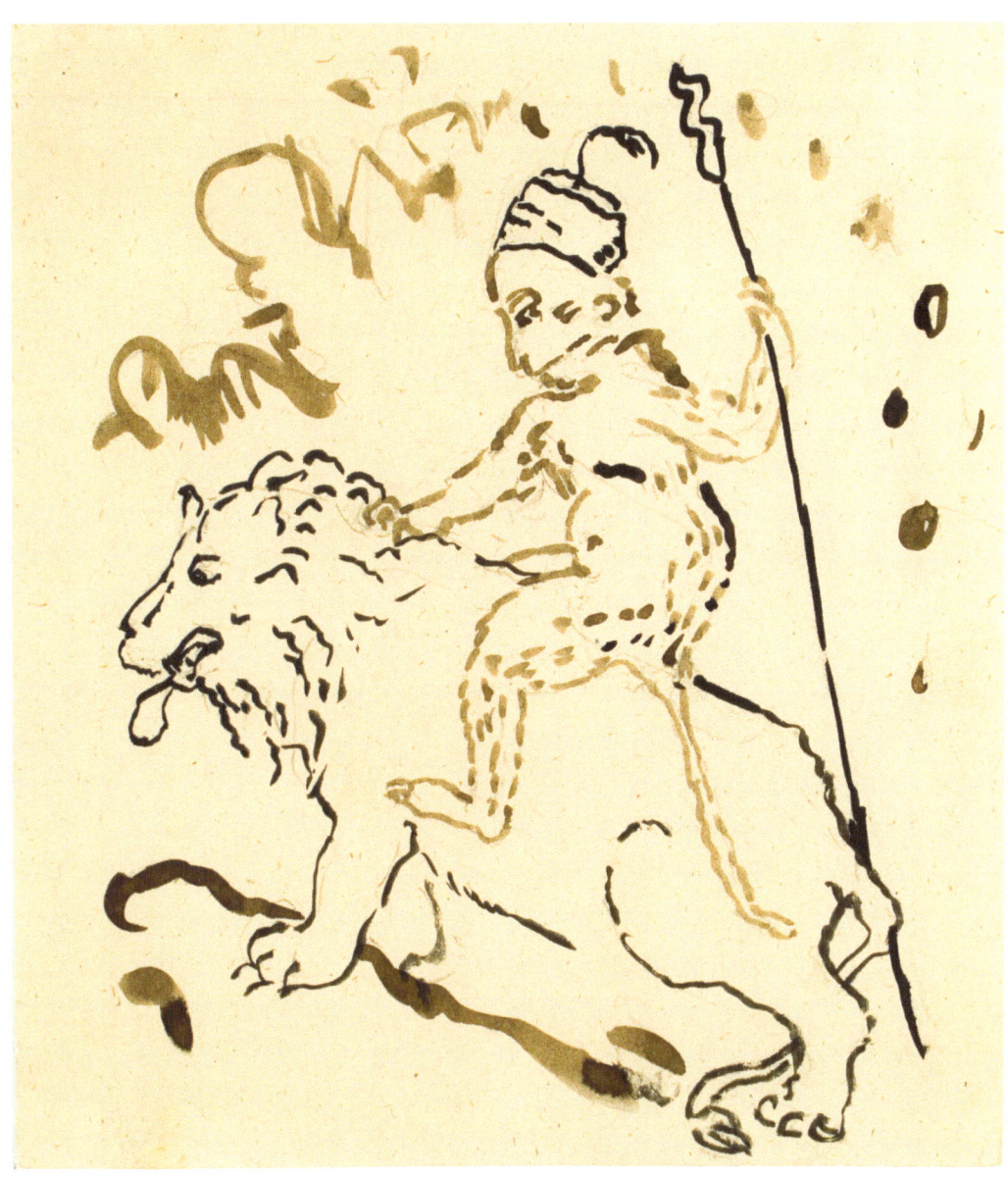

They Observe the Forest Spirit's Rights

"Modern people use the term rights, but traditional societies have different names for it. Among them, is animism. Indigenous people believe the forest is protected by spirits. We could say they observe the forest spirits rights." —Mr. Cher Wat, University of Thailand

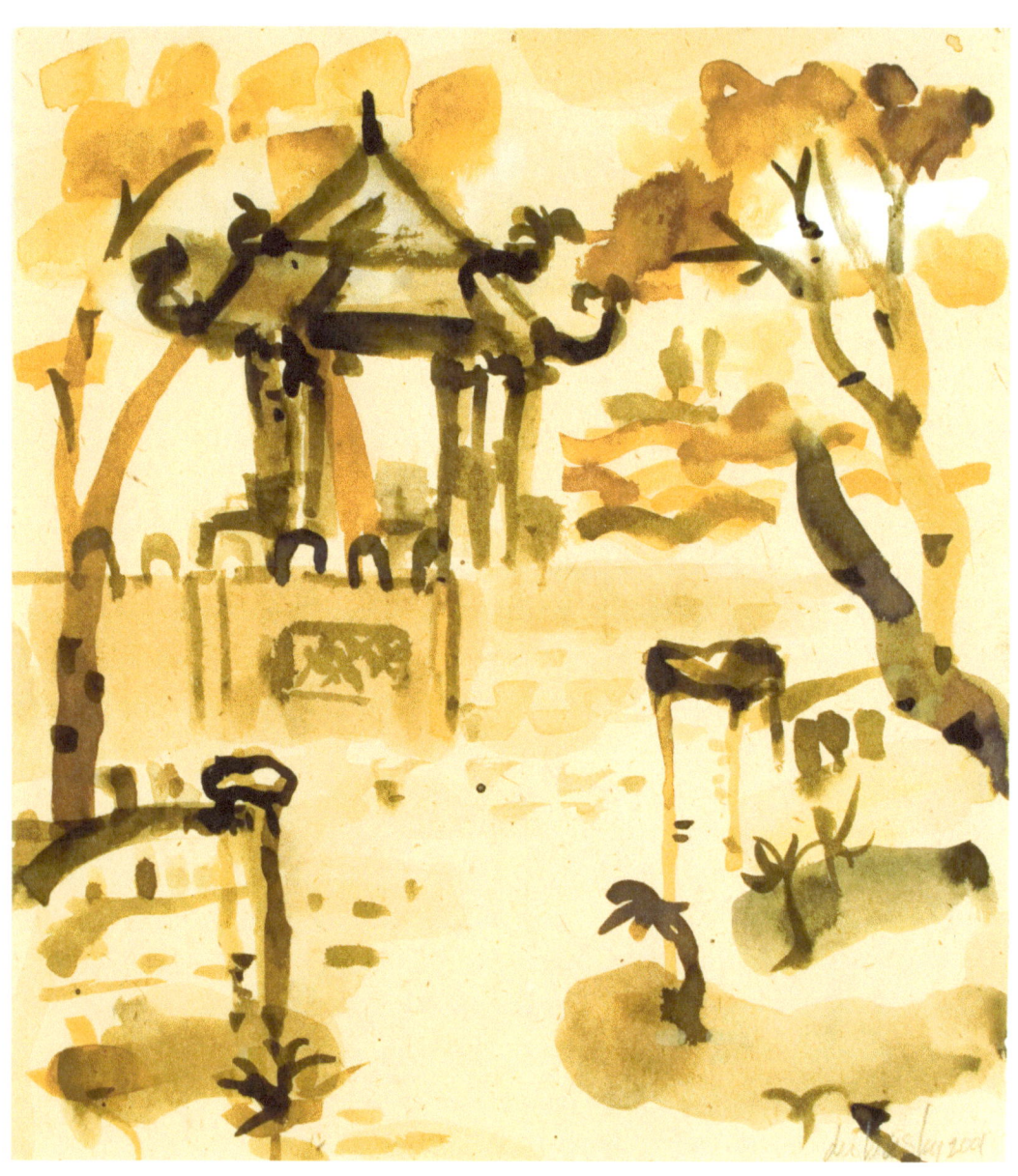

A Temple in Luong Prabang, Laos

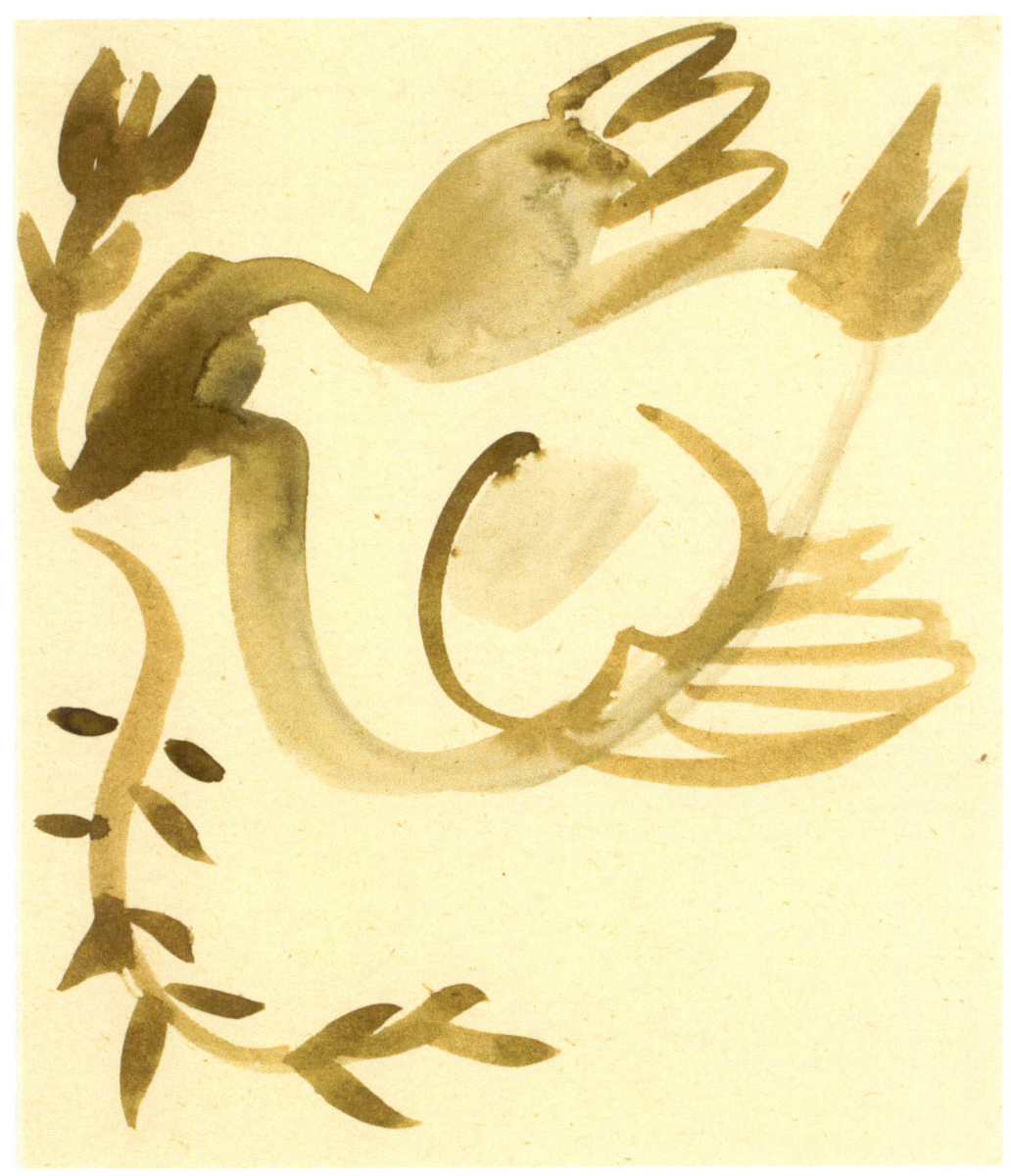

Peace Dove
"Our journey for peace begins today and everyday. Slowly, slowly, each step
is a prayer, each step is a meditation, each step will build a bridge."
—Venerable Samdech Preah Maha Ghosananda, recipient of the 15th Niwano World Peace Prize

CHRONOLOGY OF CAMBODIAN HISTORY

802 AD	The Kingdom of Angkor is established.
800 – 1400	The Angkor Civilization expands to include all of Cambodia, southeastern Thailand and northern Vietnam. It is renowned for its beautiful temples and sculpture.
1300 – 1800	Angkor declines and loses territory to the Thais and the Vietnamese. The ruined temples of Angkor Wat are buried in the jungle.
1863	Cambodia becomes a protectorate of France. French colonial rule lasts for 90 years.
1941	Prince Norodom Sihanouk is appointed king of Cambodia by the French.
1941 – 1945	Cambodia is occupied by Japan during World War II.
1946	France reimposes its protectorate.
1949 – 1952	Saloth Sar (Pol Pot) goes to Paris to study and becomes immersed in communist ideology.
Nov. 1953	Sihanouk wins the campaign for Cambodian independence from France. The Kingdom of Cambodia is established under King Sihanouk.
1963	Saloth Sar becomes General-Secretary of the Communist Party of Kampuchea (CPK).
1965	Sihanouk ends diplomatic relations with the United States amid United States and South Vietnamese border incursions into Cambodian territory and ground fighting between the Army of the Republic of Vietnam (ARVAN) troops and the Vietnamese national Liberation Front (NLF) in the Cambodian border areas.
1969	President Nixon begins an illegal, secret bombing of neutral Cambodia. An estimated 100,000 Cambodians lose their lives and two million people become homeless. The bombing continues until August 1973 when the United States Congress stops the Pentagon.
March 1970	General Lon Nol deposes King Sihanouk with United States support. Sihanouk sets up a government-in-exile in Beijing and forms an alliance with the Khmer Rouge led by Pol Pot.

April 1970	United States and South Vietnamese troops invade Cambodia to attack North Vietnamese bases and supply lines. The troops withdraw two months later.
1970 – 1975	Civil war erupts between the Khmer Rouge and the pro-American Lon Nol government. The Khmer Rouge gains support in the countryside. Rural people flee to the cities to escape the war and bombing.
April 17, 1975	The Khmer Rouge captures Phnom Penh. The Lon Nol government surrenders.
1975 – 1979	The Khmer Rouge declares "Year Zero" and imposes a radical form of agrarian communism. The cities are evacuated and the entire population is forced into slave labor. Educated people, Buddhist monks, ethnic Vietnamese, Chinese and Cham minorities are systematically massacred in an act of genocide. At least 1.7 million people die from torture, execution, starvation or disease.
1976	Cambodia is renamed Democratic Kampuchea and is cut off from the outside world. Sihanouk resigns and Khieu Samphan becomes head of state. Pol Pol becomes prime minister.
1977	Hun Sen and other Khmer Rouge officers defect to Vietnam.
Dec. 1978	Vietnam invades Cambodia following Khmer Rouge border attacks. Phnom Penh falls to the Vietnamese in two weeks. The ousted Khmer Rouge, including Pol Pot and Nuon Chea, flee to the jungle along the Thailand-Cambodia border. Pol Pot is last seen by outsiders.
Jan. 1979	The Vietnamese install a new communist government, the People's Republic of Kampuchea, led by Cambodians Hun Sen and Heng Samrin.
1979	Cambodian survivors, returnees and internally displaced people search for their lost family members. Hundreds of thousands of Cambodians flee to Thai refugee camps. The United States gives the Khmer Rouge coalition millions of dollars in aid while enforcing an international trade embargo against the Vietnamese-backed Cambodian government. The Khmer Rouge is voted, with US support, Cambodia's official representative in the United Nations.
1982	The new Vietnamese-backed Cambodian government is opposed by a coalition of three rebel groups; FUNCINPEC, the royalist group loyal to King Sihanouk; the Khmer People's national Liberation Front (KPNLF); and the Khmer Rouge.
1985	Hun Sen becomes prime minister. The Cambodian army with Vietnamese troops drive the resistance coalition into Thailand.

1980 – 1989	Cambodia enters a decade of guerrilla warfare between the Khmer Rouge coalition and the Vietnamese-sponsored government.
Sept. 1989	Vietnamese troops withdraw from Cambodia. Hun Sen abandons socialism and appeals to foreign investment. The country is renamed the State of Cambodia and Buddhism is reestablished as the state religion. The resistance coalition launches military offensives. Tens of thousands of people are displaced by fighting and landmines within Cambodia.
July 1990	The United States initiates diplomatic contact with Vietnam and Cambodia.
Oct. 1991	The United Nations Security Council brokers a peace plan that is signed by the Cambodian government and the three resistance coalition members (Khmer Rouge, Lon Nolists and FUNCINPEC). Sihanouk becomes head of state.
March 1992	United Nations peacekeepers are deployed to Cambodia to supervise the revival of Cambodia's constitutional monarchy. The United Nations Transitional Authority in Cambodia (UNTAC), that includes nearly 17,000 troops and more than 5,000 civilians, is established to disarm rebel factions, repatriate refugees, and administer democratic elections. Tens of thousands of people remain displaced, the economy is in ruins and the countryside is littered with as many as 10 million landmines.
1992	The Khmer Rouge continues to control parts of Cambodia and supports itself from the black market sale of gems and hardwoods along the border with Thailand. The Khmer Rouge refuses to disarm or cooperate with UNTAC. The United States lifts its trade embargo.
1992	The first annual Dhammayietra Peace Walk takes place during the historic repatriation of refugees from the Thai border camps. The walk is led by Maha Ghosananda, the "Gandhi of Cambodia" and is joined by Buddhist months, nuns and lay people who support the peace process.
1992	UNESCO establishes the Temples of Angkor as a World Heritage Site.
March 1993	The Khmer Rouge massacres ethnic Vietnamese living in Cambodia. Thousands of ethnic Vietnamese flee to Vietnam.
May 1993	An UNTAC sponsored general election for the National Assembly is held. Eighty-five percent of eligible Cambodians vote. The Khmer Rouge boycotts the elections. The FUNCINPEC party wins the majority of seats. Hun Sen's Cambodian People's Party (CPP), who wins the second largest number of seats, refuses to give up power. A compromise is reached and a government is formed

with two prime ministers. Prince Norodom Ranariddh of FUNCINPEC is the first prime minister and Hun Sen is the deputy prime minister. The government-in-exile loses its seat at the UN.

1993   The country is renamed the Kingdom of Cambodia. A new constitution is adopted, the monarchy is restored and Sihanouk becomes king again. Cambodia is readmitted to the international community. The Khmer Rouge wages war against the government.

Aug. 1996   The Khmer Rouge leader Ieng Sary is granted a royal pardon. Almost half of the remaining Khmer Rouge forces surrender to the government and receive amnesty.

1997   Hun Sen stages a coup against the prime minister, Prince Ranariddh, and replaces him with Ung Huot. The coup delays Cambodia's membership into the Association of Southeast Asian Nations (ASEAN).

1998   As pressure to arrest Pol Pot mounts, the Khmer Rouge holds a trial of Pol Pot and places him under house arrest. The United States seeks extradition of Pol Pot. The day before he is to be handed over, Pol Pot dies near Anlong Veng, along the Cambodian-Thailand border. Thousands of Khmer Rouge soldiers defect.

July 1998   Cambodia holds a national election. The election is won by Hun Sen's Cambodian People's Party (CPP). A coalition is formed between the CPP and FUNCINPEC with Hun Sen as prime minister and Ranariddh as president of the National Assembly.

1999   Khmer Rouge leaders Khieu Samphan, the Khmer Rouge's official representative and spokesman, and Nuon Chea, "Brother Number 2", who played a critical role in the Khmer Rouge purges, are allowed to re-enter Cambodian society. They live freely in Pailin, a former Khmer Rouge stronghold in Northwestern Cambodia along the Thailand-Cambodian border. Two Khmer Rouge leaders, Ta Mok, known as "The Butcher", and Kaing Khek Ieu (Duch), the head of Phnom Penh's notorious Tuol Sleng Prison, are placed in custody and charged with genocide.

2001   Cambodia's Senate approves a law to prosecute former leaders of the Khmer Rouge government accused of genocide.

2003   Hun Sen is reelected prime minister.

2003	The Cambodian government and the United Nations agree on a tribunal to try former Khmer Rouge leaders for crimes against humanity.
Oct. 2004	King Sihanouk abdicates and is succeeded by his son Norodom Sihamoni.
2006	The United Nations and the government of Cambodia reach an agreement on the International Tribunal to bring Khmer Rouge leaders to trial. Ta Mok dies at age 80.
2007	Khmer Rouge leaders Nuon Chea, Ieng Sary, his wife and Khieu Samphan are arrested and charged with crimes against humanity.
2008	Hun Sen's ruling Cambodian People's Party wins a majority in parliamentary elections. Cambodia and Thailand exchange rocket fire on land near the ancient Preah Vihear Temple, which is claimed by both nations. Officials from both states start talks to resolve the standoff.
2009	Duch, head of the Khmer Rouge's notorious Tuol Sleng prison, goes on trial in Phnom Penh. He is accused of presiding over the murder and torture of thousands of people.

INDEX OF COLOR PLATES

BIOGRAPHY

Artist Valentina DuBasky's paintings and prints have been included in over 130 exhibitions nationally and internationally. She is represented in numerous public collections including: *The Herbert F. Johnson Museum at Cornell University, The Newark Museum, The Orlando Museum, The Seattle Museum, The Jane Voorhees Zimmerli Art Museum, The Pew Charitable Trust Collection, The Prudential Collection, The IBM Collection, The Fuzhou International Center in China* and in private collections in Europe, Asia and the Mideast. Included in *Who's Who* and *Who's Who in American Art,* she has exhibited at United States Embassies in Estonia, Iceland, Jordan, Latvia, the Republic of the Marshall Islands, Norway, Oman, Panama, Peru and Thailand through the Art in Embassy Program, US Department of State. For more information, or to view DuBasky's paintings, prints and projects, visit www.valentinadubasky.com.

Ms. DuBasky first visited Cambodia in 1991, two months after the cease-fire was signed. In 1994, she lived in Cambodia and worked as the photographer on an oral history book about women and children survivors of the Khmer Rouge (*Soul Survivors: Stories of Women and Children in Cambodia* by Bhavia Carol Wagner with 64 photographs by Valentina DuBasky, published by Creative Arts Books, Berkeley, 2002; reprinted by Wild Iris Press, Oregon, 2007). In 1994, she produced *To Plant Seeds; To Gather Wood: Landmines in Cambodia,* a traveling, educational exhibition of her text and photographs documenting the impact of landmines on once stable communities in Cambodia. In 1998, Ms. DuBasky served as an official election observer of the Cambodian National Elections and received UN training with 600 observers from 34 countries.

She is the Founder and Executive Director of Art in a Box, (www.artinabox.org), a 501 (c) (3) nonprofit organization that assists children at risk around the world through art and art education. She resides in New York City.

Paintings by Valentina DuBasky

For more information, or to view DuBasky's paintings, prints and projects, visit www.valentinadubasky.com.

Fine Art Publications

Riverbirds and Rainforests: Valentina DuBasky
Author J.D. Talasek
Publisher National Academy of Sciences, Washington, D.C, 2005
Smithsonian Institution Libraries, Smithsonian Research Information System

Cambodian Titles

Soul Survivors - Stories of Women and Children in Cambodia
Author Bhavia C. Wagner, Valentina DuBasky (Photographer)
Publisher Wild Iris Press, Eugene, Oregon, 2008
Soul Survivors gives voice to women and children in Cambodia who survived the genocide (1975-1979), when nearly two million people died from execution, starvation, or disease. Through their detailed personal stories, 14 people reveal the brutality of Pol Pot's regime, how they managed to survive, and what it took to rebuild their lives.

Painting Our Lives: Art by Children Affected by AIDS, Children with AIDS and AIDS Orphans in Cambodia
Author Valentina DuBasky
Publisher Heron-on-Hudson Press, New York, 2008
Painting Our Lives is a book of art and testimony by Cambodian children who are living in the midst of the AIDS epidemic. Through their paintings and testimony, the children explore their identities, describe their daily lives, engage their imaginations and talk about their dreams for the future. *Painting Our Lives* places the paintings and testimony by these remarkable and inspiring young people into the historical record of AIDS in our times.

Art in a Box

Art in a Box partners with communities around the world that are in need, disadvantaged by poverty, or that are facing crisis situations due to war, public health emergencies or natural disasters, and assists in recovery and empowerment through art. We respect the depth and diversity of people who are often viewed as representatives of their circumstances rather than as unique individuals. Art in a Box is a 501(c)(3) tax-exempt, non-profit organization. For more information, visit www.artinabox.org.

www.ingramcontent.com/pod-product-compliance
Lightning Source LLC
Chambersburg PA
CBHW050751180526
45159CB00003B/1428